Social Media Manipulation Techniques

By Leslie Che

Contents

Introduction

Definition and Overview of Manipulation on Social Media

In today's hyper-connected world, social media platforms are more than just tools for communication and self-expression—they have become powerful forces capable of shaping opinions, influencing behaviours, and even altering the course of events. From the subtle nudging of your news feed to the more overt tactics used in political campaigns, manipulation on social media is a pervasive reality that many users remain largely unaware of.

But what exactly is manipulation in the context of social media? At its core, manipulation refers to the deliberate use of digital tools, content, and algorithms to influence users' actions, opinions, and emotions. This can range from personalised advertising designed to trigger impulsive purchases to more insidious techniques aimed at promoting disinformation, exploiting vulnerabilities, or steering societal discourse. Whether it's by pushing specific content, suppressing dissenting voices, or creating echo chambers, social media manipulation operates at the intersection of technology, psychology, and corporate interests.

Understanding how manipulation works on social media is crucial for users to make informed decisions about their online behaviour, consumption habits, and how they engage with content. It also highlights the need for broader discussions around ethics, transparency, and accountability in the digital age.

The Power of Algorithms: How Social Media Influences Behaviour

At the heart of social media's ability to manipulate is the algorithm. These complex, data-driven systems determine what users see, when they see it, and how frequently content is shown. On platforms like Facebook, Twitter, Instagram, and YouTube, algorithms decide which posts appear in your feed, which ads are targeted at you, and which videos are suggested for you to watch next.

Algorithms are designed to maximise engagement. They analyse users' behaviour, interests, and interactions to keep them scrolling, clicking, liking, and sharing for as long as possible. The more time spent on the platform, the more data is collected, and the more effective the algorithms become at predicting and influencing user behaviour. This leads to a feedback loop where users are constantly fed content that reinforces their preferences, beliefs, and emotions.

While this may seem harmless, the manipulative nature of algorithms becomes evident when considering how they are used to drive advertising revenue and influence opinions. For example, platforms may prioritise sensational or emotionally charged content because it triggers more engagement, even if it's misleading or harmful. By favouring divisive material, social media algorithms can amplify polarisation, create echo chambers, and distort perceptions of reality.

In essence, users are not always in control of what they see; their online experience is shaped by hidden forces designed to capitalise on their attention, desires, and fears. This power to subtly manipulate user behaviour raises important questions about autonomy and the impact of social media on society at large.

The Ethical Debate: Free Will vs. Manipulation

One of the most significant ethical dilemmas surrounding social media manipulation is the tension between free will and influence. While platforms are quick to emphasise user choice and personal responsibility, the sophisticated nature of their manipulative tools challenges the notion of true autonomy online. Are users genuinely making decisions based on their own free will, or are they being steered towards particular actions and beliefs through calculated design?

For instance, personalised ads exploit psychological triggers, using data about users' emotions, habits, and desires to push them towards specific purchases or decisions. Similarly, political campaigns use micro-targeting techniques to influence voters in highly tailored ways, often without their awareness. In both cases, the line between persuasion and manipulation becomes blurred.

Moreover, the ethical concerns extend beyond individual users to society as a whole. When social media platforms are used to spread disinformation or sway public opinion, the consequences can be far-reaching, impacting democratic processes, social cohesion, and even public health, as seen during the COVID-19 pandemic.

Critics argue that these platforms have a responsibility to curb manipulative practices and protect users from exploitation. Advocates of digital freedom, on the other hand, maintain that individuals should have the right to make their own choices, even in a landscape heavily influenced by algorithms and data-driven content.

As we continue to navigate the complexities of the digital age, the ethical debate surrounding social media manipulation will remain a critical issue. Understanding how manipulation works—and recognising when it is happening—is the first step towards reclaiming agency in an increasingly controlled online environment.

In the chapters ahead, we will delve deeper into the various techniques used to manipulate users on social media, from the psychology behind persuasive design to the role of influencers and bots in shaping discourse. By examining these tactics, we aim to equip readers with the knowledge needed to critically engage with social media platforms and better understand the forces at play in the digital world.

Chapter 1: The Psychology of Social Media Manipulation

1.1 The Science of Influence: Understanding Human Behaviour Online

At the core of social media manipulation lies a deep understanding of human psychology. Social media platforms, by their very nature, are designed to exploit the behavioural and cognitive patterns that govern our actions and decisions. These platforms leverage principles of psychology—such as social proof, reciprocity, and the need for validation—to subtly influence how we interact with content and, in turn, how we think, feel, and behave online.

Humans are naturally social creatures, hardwired to seek connection and affirmation from others. Social media taps into these instincts by creating an environment where likes, shares, and comments serve as forms of social validation. This validation is addictive; the more feedback we receive, the more we crave it, leading to increased time spent on the platform and heightened vulnerability to manipulation.

1.2 Dopamine and the Reward System

One of the most powerful psychological mechanisms exploited by social media is the brain's reward system. Dopamine, a neurotransmitter associated with pleasure and reward, plays a key role in our response to social media. Each notification, like, or share triggers a small release of dopamine, reinforcing the desire to check our phones and engage with content.

This intermittent reinforcement, similar to what is used in gambling, creates a cycle of addiction. Users are constantly seeking the next "hit" of dopamine, and platforms design their notifications, scrolling features, and user interfaces to maximise this effect. The constant craving for validation and engagement makes users more susceptible to manipulation, as they become less mindful of the content they consume and more driven by the rewards of interaction.

1.3 The Fear of Missing Out (FOMO)

FOMO, or the Fear of Missing Out, is another powerful psychological force that social media platforms exploit to keep users engaged. Social media thrives on the notion of constant connectivity, where users are bombarded with updates, trends, and events in real-time. The fear of missing out on important information or social interactions compels users to stay online, often leading to compulsive checking and scrolling.

This fear is heightened by the curated nature of social media feeds. Platforms show users the most engaging and attention-grabbing content, often from friends or influencers who seem to be living idealised lives. This creates a sense of inadequacy and comparison, driving users to remain connected in the hope of not missing out on experiences, trends, or connections that seem essential to social status and belonging.

FOMO is a powerful tool of manipulation, encouraging users to engage more frequently, making them more vulnerable to targeted advertising, misinformation, and other manipulative tactics.

1.4 Social Proof: The Power of Group Influence

Social proof is a well-established psychological phenomenon that describes how individuals tend to conform to the behaviour of others, especially in uncertain situations. In the context of social media, social proof manifests through the number of likes, shares, and comments a post receives. When users see that a particular piece of content has garnered significant attention, they are more likely to engage with it as well, assuming its popularity is a marker of credibility or value.

This creates a feedback loop where highly engaging content becomes more visible, regardless of its quality or accuracy. Manipulative actors, such as advertisers, influencers, or political entities, can exploit social proof by artificially inflating engagement through bots or paid likes, making their content appear more trustworthy or popular than it really is.

The power of social proof extends beyond individual posts to broader trends and movements. For example, viral challenges, hashtags, or political campaigns can gain momentum through the snowball effect of social proof, encouraging users to participate simply because "everyone else is doing it." This herd mentality makes social media users susceptible to manipulation, as they may engage with content or adopt behaviours without critically evaluating their motivations or the content's authenticity.

1.5 Confirmation Bias and Echo Chambers

One of the most significant ways social media manipulates users is by exploiting confirmation bias—the tendency to seek out and favour information that aligns with our pre-existing beliefs and values. Social media platforms use algorithms that track user preferences and interactions, serving content that reinforces users' existing viewpoints. This creates echo chambers, where individuals are only exposed to information that confirms their beliefs, while opposing perspectives are filtered out or minimised.

Echo chambers amplify the effects of confirmation bias, leading to polarisation, groupthink, and a distorted perception of reality. Users in these closed-off environments become more confident in their beliefs, even if they are misinformed or manipulated by external actors. This makes it easier for manipulative entities, such as fake news creators or political operatives, to target users with biased content that fuels division and strengthens existing biases.

The result is a more polarised and less informed society, where critical thinking is eroded, and individuals are more likely to engage with manipulative content that plays to their fears, desires, or ideological leanings.

1.6 Scarcity and Urgency: Creating a Sense of Pressure

Scarcity and urgency are classic psychological tactics used in advertising and sales, but they are also widely employed on social media. Scarcity refers to the perception that a resource or opportunity is limited, while urgency creates the impression that immediate action is required to avoid missing out. These tactics are used to manipulate users into making quick decisions without fully considering the consequences.

On social media, scarcity and urgency are often seen in the form of limited-time offers, flash sales, or exclusive content. Influencers and brands use phrases like "only available for 24 hours" or "limited stock remaining" to create a sense of urgency and pressure users into taking immediate action. This manipulative technique plays on the fear of missing out and the human tendency to prioritise short-term rewards over long-term considerations.

Beyond e-commerce, scarcity and urgency can be used in social movements, political campaigns, or viral challenges, where users feel pressured to engage quickly before they miss the chance to be part of something important or exclusive. This tactic manipulates behaviour by overriding rational decision-making processes, encouraging impulsive actions based on fear and desire.

1.7 Emotional Manipulation: The Role of Content Design

Emotional manipulation is another powerful tool used by social media platforms and content creators to influence user behaviour. Posts that elicit strong emotional reactions—whether positive or negative—are more likely to be shared and engaged with, as emotions play a key role in driving human behaviour. Social media algorithms prioritise emotionally charged content because it generates higher levels of interaction, keeping users on the platform longer.

Manipulative actors often use fear, anger, joy, or sadness to influence users. For example, sensationalist headlines, fear-mongering posts, or heartwarming stories can trigger emotional responses that bypass critical thinking and rational analysis. Users are more likely to engage with content that evokes a strong emotional reaction, making them vulnerable to manipulation by individuals or organisations seeking to push a particular agenda.

This emotional manipulation is further amplified by the design of social media platforms, which use bright colours, notifications, and animations to stimulate emotional responses and encourage addictive behaviour. By appealing to users' emotions, social media manipulates behaviour in ways that benefit the platform's engagement metrics while often disregarding the well-being of its users.

In this chapter, we have explored how social media platforms use psychological principles to manipulate user behaviour, from exploiting dopamine-driven reward systems to leveraging social proof and emotional manipulation. By understanding these tactics, users can begin to recognise when they are being manipulated and take steps to regain control over their online experiences.

In the next chapter, **Chapter 2: The Role of Algorithms in Shaping User Experiences**, we will dive deeper into how algorithms dictate what users see, how they interact with content, and how they can be exploited for manipulative purposes.

Chapter 2: The Role of Algorithms in Shaping User Experiences

2.1 Introduction to Algorithms in Social Media

At the heart of every social media platform lies a powerful, often invisible, force: algorithms. These complex sets of rules and calculations determine nearly everything users see on their feeds—from posts and advertisements to suggested friends and trending topics. Social media algorithms curate and organise vast amounts of data, creating personalised user experiences designed to increase engagement and keep users online longer.

However, while algorithms offer convenience and efficiency, they also wield significant power over users' online experiences. By controlling the content users see, algorithms shape behaviour, influence opinions, and even manipulate emotional states. This chapter explores how algorithms operate, their impact on user experiences, and how they can be used for manipulative purposes.

2.2 How Social Media Algorithms Work

Social media platforms are inundated with content. Without algorithms, users would be overwhelmed by the sheer volume of information. To make this data manageable and relevant, algorithms sort through it, using various factors to decide what appears at the top of a user's feed. These factors include:

- **User Preferences and Behaviour**: Algorithms track and analyse each user's activity—what they like, comment on, share, and spend time viewing. This data informs the algorithm about the user's interests, which in turn dictates what content is prioritised.

- **Engagement Metrics**: Posts that generate high levels of engagement (likes, shares, comments) are often boosted by algorithms, increasing their visibility. This creates a feedback loop where popular content becomes even more popular, regardless of its substance or accuracy.

- **Relevance and Recency**: Algorithms give preference to recent and trending content. If a post is timely and relevant to current events, it is more likely to be featured prominently in users' feeds.

- **Social Connections**: The closer a user is to someone in their network (based on interactions, mutual friends, etc.), the more likely they are to see that person's content. This reinforces existing social circles and relationships.

- **Paid Content**: Sponsored posts and advertisements are given preferential treatment by algorithms, ensuring they are seen by as many users as possible.

These factors collectively influence what users see and how they engage with content. The underlying goal for platforms is to maximise user engagement and time spent on the site—metrics that are often in conflict with providing balanced or unbiased content.

2.3 The Filter Bubble: Customising Content, Limiting Perspectives

One of the most significant consequences of algorithm-driven feeds is the creation of "filter bubbles." A filter bubble occurs when algorithms curate content that aligns closely with a user's preferences, limiting exposure to diverse viewpoints. As algorithms prioritise content similar to what users have previously engaged with, over time, individuals are isolated within echo chambers of information that reflect their existing beliefs and interests.

While this can enhance user satisfaction in the short term, it has long-term consequences. Filter bubbles reinforce confirmation bias, where users are only exposed to content that validates their opinions. This selective exposure can lead to polarisation, making users more resistant to opposing perspectives and less likely to engage in critical thinking.

For manipulative actors, filter bubbles provide fertile ground for spreading misinformation, propaganda, or biased content. By targeting specific demographic or ideological groups, these actors can exploit algorithms to amplify divisive content, further entrenching polarisation within society.

2.4 The Algorithmic Amplification of Extreme Content

One of the unintended consequences of algorithmic curation is the amplification of extreme or sensational content. Social media platforms rely on engagement metrics to determine what content is promoted. Posts that evoke strong emotional reactions—such as anger, fear, or outrage—tend to generate higher engagement, as users are more likely to comment, share, or respond to such content.

Algorithms, in their quest to keep users engaged, often prioritise emotionally charged content over more nuanced or balanced posts. This creates a cycle where extreme views, sensationalist headlines, and emotionally manipulative content dominate the platform, drowning out moderate or rational discussions.

This amplification of extreme content has significant societal implications. It can distort users' perceptions of reality, making them believe that extreme viewpoints are more widespread or accepted than they actually are. Additionally, it can drive polarisation and divisiveness, as users are more likely to interact with content that fuels outrage or fear.

2.5 Manipulating User Behaviour Through Algorithmic Design

Algorithms don't just determine what users see—they also shape how users behave. Platforms use algorithmic design to nudge users towards specific actions, whether it's liking a post, clicking on a link, or making a purchase. These subtle manipulations are often hidden from users, but they significantly influence decision-making and online behaviour.

Some of the ways in which algorithms manipulate user behaviour include:

- **Content Prioritisation**: Algorithms push certain posts to the top of a user's feed, encouraging interaction with those posts over others. This gives platforms control over which ideas and narratives gain prominence.

- **Infinite Scrolling**: Platforms design their interfaces to keep users engaged. Features like infinite scrolling, where new content continuously loads, make it easy for users to lose track of time and stay on the platform longer. This keeps users exposed to more content and advertisements, increasing their vulnerability to manipulation.

- **Targeted Advertisements**: Algorithms use detailed profiles of user behaviour and preferences to deliver highly targeted ads. These ads are often tailored to exploit emotional vulnerabilities or appeal to specific desires, making users more likely to make impulsive purchases or decisions.

- **Personalised Recommendations**: By recommending content based on past behaviour, algorithms can subtly steer users towards specific types of content. Over time, this personalisation can shape users' interests and opinions, narrowing their range of exposure and limiting their autonomy in choosing what they engage with.

These algorithmic techniques are powerful because they operate at a subconscious level. Users may feel they are in control of their online experience, but in reality, their actions are often guided by the algorithms that dictate what they see and how they interact.

2.6 Exploiting Algorithms for Manipulative Purposes

While algorithms are designed to enhance user experiences and engagement, they can also be exploited for more nefarious purposes. Manipulative actors—such as advertisers, political operatives, or even nation-states—can game algorithms to spread misinformation, influence public opinion, or manipulate consumer behaviour.

Some common techniques used to exploit algorithms include:

- **Bot Networks**: Bots are automated accounts that can be programmed to like, share, or comment on specific content. By artificially boosting engagement, bots can trick algorithms into promoting certain posts or accounts, making them appear more popular or credible than they are.

- **Clickbait**: Sensationalist headlines and misleading thumbnails are often used to lure users into clicking on content. Clickbait takes advantage of algorithms' preference for high engagement by generating clicks through misleading or emotionally charged content.

- **Fake News and Misinformation**: Misinformation campaigns rely on the viral nature of social media algorithms to spread false or misleading information. By exploiting the algorithmic amplification of sensational content, fake news can quickly reach millions of users, shaping public opinion and distorting reality.

- **Astroturfing**: Astroturfing refers to the practice of creating fake grassroots movements or artificially inflating support for a cause. By using bots or paid actors to engage with content, manipulative actors can trick algorithms into amplifying their message, making it appear as though there is widespread public support for their agenda.

These techniques exploit the very mechanisms that social media platforms use to keep users engaged. As a result, manipulative actors can bypass traditional gatekeepers of information, such as journalists or regulators, and directly influence the public in ways that are difficult to detect or counter.

2.7 The Ethics of Algorithmic Manipulation

The widespread use of algorithms to manipulate user behaviour raises important ethical questions. On one hand, algorithms can enhance user experiences by delivering personalised content and recommendations. On the other hand, they can also be used to exploit psychological vulnerabilities, spread misinformation, and distort public discourse.

One of the key ethical concerns is the issue of transparency. Most users are unaware of how algorithms work or how their behaviour is being shaped by the content they see. This lack of transparency undermines users' autonomy and raises questions about whether platforms are acting in the best interests of their users.

Another ethical concern is the role of algorithms in amplifying harmful content. By prioritising engagement over accuracy or quality, platforms may inadvertently promote content that fuels division, misinformation, or extremism. This can have serious consequences for democratic processes, social cohesion, and individual well-being.

2.8 Towards Greater Algorithmic Accountability

As the role of algorithms in shaping user experiences becomes more prominent, there is growing demand for greater accountability and transparency from social media platforms. Some steps that could be taken to address the ethical concerns surrounding algorithms include:

- **Algorithmic Transparency**: Platforms should provide users with clear information about how algorithms work and what factors influence the content they see. This could include explanations of how posts are ranked, what data is used to personalise feeds, and how engagement metrics are calculated.

- **User Control**: Users should have more control over their online experiences. This could include the ability to customise their feeds, opt out of algorithmic personalisation, or access content in chronological order rather than algorithmically ranked order.

- **Regulation and Oversight**: Governments and regulatory bodies may need to step in to ensure that platforms are not using algorithms to manipulate users in harmful ways. This could involve creating standards for algorithmic transparency, requiring platforms to address the spread of misinformation, or limiting the use of manipulative design techniques.

In this chapter, we have explored the powerful role that algorithms play in shaping user experiences on social media. From filter bubbles and echo chambers to the amplification of extreme content, algorithms have a profound impact on how we interact with the digital world. Understanding these mechanisms is essential for recognising when and how we are being manipulated.

In the next chapter, **Chapter 3: Data as Currency: How Social Media Platforms Monetise User Behaviour**, we will explore the ways in which user data is collected, sold, and used to generate profits—and how this process can be exploited for manipulative purposes.

Chapter 3: Data as Currency: How Social Media Platforms Monetise User Behaviour

3.1 Introduction to Data Monetisation in Social Media

In the digital age, data has become one of the most valuable assets. For social media platforms, user data—ranging from personal information to browsing habits and interactions—serves as the primary currency. Platforms collect vast amounts of this data, which they then use to personalise user experiences, serve targeted advertisements, and ultimately, generate significant profits.

However, the commodification of personal data raises numerous ethical concerns. Users often have little understanding or control over how their data is collected, shared, or sold. Furthermore, data monetisation can lead to exploitative practices, with social media platforms and third parties using sophisticated techniques to manipulate user behaviour for profit. In this chapter, we will examine the mechanisms behind data collection, how it is monetised, and the potential for exploitation.

3.2 The Mechanics of Data Collection

Social media platforms gather a wide array of data from their users. This includes:

- **Personal Information**: Basic details like names, ages, locations, and contact information are collected when users create accounts. This data forms the foundation of the user profile that platforms use to target content and ads.

- **User Behaviour**: Platforms track how users interact with content—what posts they like, share, or comment on, how long they spend on certain pages, and which profiles they engage with most frequently. This behaviour data is invaluable for building detailed user profiles.

- **Browsing Habits**: Through cookies and other tracking technologies, social media platforms can monitor users' browsing activity even outside of their platforms. This allows them to build comprehensive profiles that include users' shopping habits, search histories, and website visits.

- **Location Data**: Many social media platforms track users' real-time locations through their devices. This data can be used to personalise content or serve geographically relevant advertisements, but it also raises significant privacy concerns.

- **Device Information**: Platforms can gather data on the devices users access their platforms from—such as smartphones, tablets, or computers. This includes the type of device, operating system, and even technical details like IP addresses, which can help pinpoint a user's location.

All of this data is valuable because it provides platforms and advertisers with insights into users' preferences, habits, and lifestyles, enabling them to deliver highly targeted and personalised content. However, it also sets the stage for potential exploitation.

3.3 How Social Media Platforms Monetise User Data

The primary way social media platforms generate revenue is through advertisements. The data they collect from users allows them to offer highly personalised and effective advertising services to businesses. Key methods of monetising user data include:

- **Targeted Advertising**: Social media platforms use the data they collect to create detailed profiles of their users. Advertisers can then pay to have their ads shown to specific audiences based on demographics, interests, behaviour, and even location. This precision targeting increases the likelihood of engagement and conversion, making the platform's ad space more valuable.

- **Data Sharing and Selling**: In some cases, social media platforms may share or sell user data to third-party companies, such as marketers, data brokers, or analytics firms. These third parties can use the data to refine their marketing strategies, develop new products, or build even more comprehensive user profiles. Although many platforms claim they anonymise or aggregate the data they sell, privacy risks remain, as even anonymous data can often be re-identified.

- **Predictive Analytics**: By analysing the vast amounts of data collected, platforms can predict user behaviour and preferences with increasing accuracy. This allows them to proactively serve ads or recommend products before users even express interest. While this can improve the user experience, it also blurs the line between marketing and manipulation, as users may be nudged towards making decisions they might not otherwise have made.

- **Influencer and Content Monetisation**: Social media platforms also monetise user-generated content by encouraging influencers and creators to engage with their audiences. Data on how users interact with content helps platforms recommend the most popular influencers and monetise their visibility through ad revenue sharing, sponsored posts, or exclusive content.

3.4 Data as a Tool for Manipulation

The data collected by social media platforms not only enables targeted advertising but also opens the door for more manipulative practices. Some of the ways data can be used to manipulate user behaviour include:

- **Microtargeting**: Microtargeting involves delivering highly specific and personalised ads or content to individuals or small groups based on detailed data profiles. Political campaigns, for example, have used microtargeting to influence voters by showing them tailored messages that appeal to their unique concerns, fears, or beliefs. This can be problematic, as users are often unaware they are being manipulated and may not critically evaluate the information presented to them.

- **Psychographic Profiling**: By combining behavioural data with psychographic data—such as personality traits, values, and motivations—platforms and advertisers can gain deeper insights into how to influence users. Psychographic profiling has been used to manipulate users' decisions, from purchasing products to changing political opinions, often without users realising they are being influenced.

- **A/B Testing and Behavioural Nudging**: Platforms frequently conduct A/B testing, where two versions of content or ads are shown to different groups of users to see which performs better. These tests allow platforms to refine their techniques for nudging user behaviour. While A/B testing is not inherently malicious, it can be used to subtly manipulate users into engaging with content or making decisions that serve the platform's or advertiser's interests.

- **Addiction by Design**: The data social media platforms collect on users' habits is often used to optimise platform design for maximum engagement. By analysing when users are most likely to log on, what content keeps them online longer, and what triggers them to return, platforms can develop strategies that encourage compulsive use. This can lead to addictive behaviours, with users spending more time on social media than intended, often at the cost of their mental health and well-being.

3.5 The Hidden Costs of "Free" Platforms

Most social media platforms are offered to users for free, but this comes with a hidden cost: users' personal data. While users may not pay in currency, they effectively "pay" with their information, which is then used to generate revenue for the platform. This exchange raises several ethical questions:

- **Informed Consent**: Many users do not fully understand what data they are giving up or how it will be used. Privacy policies are often long, complex, and filled with legal jargon, making it difficult for users to give informed consent.

- **Data Ownership**: Once users share their data with a platform, they lose control over how it is used. While some platforms allow users to delete their accounts or opt out of certain data collection practices, in many cases, the data has already been shared with third parties, making it difficult to regain

control.

- **Exploitation of Vulnerable Users**: Social media platforms often target
their services towards young people, who may be less aware of the risks
associated with data sharing. Additionally, vulnerable groups - such as those
with mental health issues or low digital literacy - may be more easily
manipulated by targeted advertising or addictive design features.

3.6 Legal and Ethical Implications of Data Monetisation

The growing awareness of data monetisation practices has sparked calls for stronger
regulation and greater transparency. In the UK and Europe, the **General Data
Protection Regulation (GDPR)** was introduced to give users more control over
their personal data and to ensure that companies handle it responsibly. GDPR
requires companies to be transparent about what data they collect, how they use it,
and gives users the right to access and delete their data.

However, despite these regulations, there are ongoing concerns about how
effectively they are enforced and whether they go far enough in addressing the
manipulative potential of data monetisation. Ethical questions about the
commodification of personal data, especially in cases where users are unaware of
how their information is being used, continue to be debated.

3.7 Navigating the Data Economy: What Can Users Do?

While regulatory efforts like GDPR are a step in the right direction, users must also take proactive steps to protect their privacy and limit the ways in which their data is exploited. Some actions users can take include:

- **Privacy Settings**: Review and adjust the privacy settings on social media platforms to limit data sharing. Many platforms offer options to control who can see your posts, what data is shared with advertisers, and how your location is tracked.

- **Limit Data Sharing**: Be cautious about sharing personal information online, especially when signing up for new platforms or services. Avoid linking social media accounts to other apps or websites unless necessary.

- **Ad-Blockers and Tracking Prevention Tools**: Consider using ad-blockers or tracking prevention tools that limit the ability of social media platforms to collect data on your browsing habits.

- **Informed Use of Social Media**: Stay informed about the data practices of the platforms you use. Reading privacy policies may not be exciting, but it can help you understand what you're agreeing to. Additionally, avoid platforms that have a history of questionable data practices.

In this chapter, we have explored the ways in which social media platforms collect, monetise, and potentially exploit user data. By understanding the mechanisms behind data collection and how it is used to generate profit, users can become more aware of the hidden costs associated with social media and take steps to protect their privacy.

In the next chapter, **Chapter 4: The Psychology of Social Media Manipulation: Exploiting Human Behaviour**, we will dive into the psychological techniques used by social media platforms and advertisers to manipulate user behaviour, including the use of dopamine-driven feedback loops and emotional manipulation.

Chapter 4: The Psychology of Social Media Manipulation: Exploiting Human Behaviour

4.1 Introduction: The Intersection of Psychology and Social Media

The success of social media platforms is not solely the result of clever algorithms or innovative design—it is deeply rooted in human psychology. By understanding the cognitive and emotional responses that drive human behaviour, social media platforms and advertisers have been able to exploit these mechanisms to increase user engagement, drive interactions, and ultimately, generate profit. In this chapter, we will explore the psychological techniques used to manipulate behaviour on social media, focusing on concepts such as **dopamine-driven feedback loops,** **emotional manipulation**, and **social validation**.

4.2 The Dopamine Loop: Reinforcing Addictive Behaviour

At the core of social media's ability to capture and hold attention is the brain's **reward system**, which is largely regulated by dopamine, a neurotransmitter that plays a key role in the brain's reward and pleasure centres. Dopamine is released in response to experiences that are perceived as rewarding, such as receiving a like, comment, or notification on social media.

4.2.1 The Science Behind Dopamine Feedback Loops

A **dopamine feedback loop** is created when an individual engages in a behaviour that triggers a pleasurable response, which in turn motivates the person to repeat that behaviour. Social media platforms are designed to exploit this loop by offering intermittent rewards—likes, shares, comments, or followers—that release bursts of dopamine, reinforcing the desire to continue engaging with the platform.

- **Intermittent Reinforcement**: Social media platforms are particularly effective because they use **intermittent reinforcement**, a psychological phenomenon where rewards are given at unpredictable intervals. This uncertainty keeps users coming back for more, as they never know when the next "hit" of dopamine will occur.

- **Notifications and Alerts**: The constant flow of notifications and alerts is designed to re-engage users throughout the day, pulling them back into the dopamine loop. Each time a user checks their phone and finds new interactions, their brain releases dopamine, reinforcing the habit.

4.2.2 The Impact of Dopamine on Addiction

The frequent release of dopamine can lead to habitual or even addictive behaviour. Users may find themselves compulsively checking their social media accounts, craving the next hit of validation or engagement. This behaviour is often reinforced by **social validation** mechanisms, such as likes and comments, which signal acceptance and approval from others.

Over time, the brain becomes conditioned to expect the constant stimulation and reward provided by social media, making it difficult for users to disengage. This can lead to negative consequences, such as **social media addiction**, which has been linked to decreased attention spans, anxiety, and depression.

4.3 Emotional Manipulation: Exploiting Users' Feelings

Social media platforms also leverage users' emotional responses to keep them engaged. By manipulating emotions—whether through the content users are exposed to or the way interactions are framed—platforms can heighten engagement and foster emotional dependencies.

4.3.1 Amplifying Emotions for Engagement

Research shows that emotionally charged content tends to evoke stronger reactions and is more likely to be shared or commented on. This is why **outrage**, **fear**, and **excitement** are common emotions exploited by social media platforms. Algorithms often prioritise content that is more likely to elicit strong emotional responses, as this increases user engagement.

- **Outrage and Fear**: Content that triggers outrage or fear is particularly effective at capturing attention. This is why platforms often promote news stories, political posts, or controversial topics that spark intense debates and emotional reactions. Such content keeps users engaged, even if it leads to negative emotions, because it creates a sense of urgency or threat.

- **Positive Reinforcement**: On the other end of the spectrum, content that elicits positive emotions—such as funny memes, heartwarming stories, or motivational posts—also increases engagement. Users are more likely to share content that makes them feel good, which in turn reinforces positive behaviour and keeps them returning for more.

4.3.2 The Role of Empathy and Mirror Neurons

Another psychological phenomenon that social media platforms exploit is **empathy**. Humans are naturally wired to empathise with others, and when users see posts that express joy, sadness, anger, or frustration, their **mirror neurons** fire, causing them to experience those emotions as if they were their own. This emotional mirroring strengthens the connection users feel with the content and encourages further interaction, whether through comments, likes, or shares.

4.4 Social Validation: The Need for Approval

Humans have an inherent need for social validation—being accepted and approved by others is deeply tied to self-esteem and identity. Social media platforms have expertly tapped into this psychological need by designing systems that reward users with likes, comments, and followers, which serve as metrics of social approval.

4.4.1 The Psychology of Likes and Shares

Likes, shares, and comments serve as public signals of social validation. When users receive positive feedback on their posts, they experience a sense of approval and self-worth, which reinforces the behaviour of sharing more content. This feedback loop becomes addictive, as users constantly seek external validation from their peers.

- **Comparing Metrics**: Social media also encourages users to compare their metrics (likes, followers, etc.) with those of others, fostering a sense of competition. This comparison can lead to feelings of inadequacy or anxiety when users perceive that they are not receiving as much social validation as others.

4.4.2 The Dark Side of Social Validation: FOMO and Self-Esteem

The constant pursuit of social validation can have negative effects on mental health. **Fear of Missing Out (FOMO)** is a common consequence, as users become anxious about missing out on events, trends, or social interactions. Additionally, the pressure to maintain an idealised online image can lead to reduced self-esteem, especially when users compare themselves to others who appear to have more likes, followers, or a more "perfect" lifestyle.

4.5 Emotional Manipulation in Advertising

Advertisers on social media platforms also use emotional manipulation to influence consumer behaviour. By targeting ads that tap into users' emotions—whether through happiness, nostalgia, fear, or guilt—advertisers can create a psychological need for their products or services.

- **Fear-Based Advertising**: Ads that evoke fear, such as those related to personal safety, health, or financial stability, are particularly effective at prompting action. By creating a sense of urgency, advertisers can manipulate users into making purchases or engaging with content.

- **Emotional Appeal**: Advertisers also use positive emotions, such as happiness or excitement, to create a positive association with their brand. For example, an ad featuring happy families or exciting travel destinations can trigger users' desires to experience those emotions themselves, leading to engagement or purchases.

4.6 The Role of AI in Emotional Manipulation

Artificial intelligence (AI) plays a significant role in emotional manipulation on social media. AI algorithms are able to analyse vast amounts of data to detect users' emotional states and predict how they will respond to different types of content. This allows platforms and advertisers to tailor content that is more likely to elicit the desired emotional response.

- **Sentiment Analysis**: AI-powered sentiment analysis tools can detect the emotions behind users' posts, comments, and interactions. This data is then used to personalise the content users see, ensuring that they are shown posts or ads that align with their emotional state.

- **Emotionally Targeted Ads**: Advertisers use AI to serve emotionally targeted ads that align with a user's current mood. For example, if a user is posting about a stressful day, they might be shown ads for relaxation products or services. This level of personalisation can increase the likelihood of engagement but also raises ethical concerns about manipulation.

4.7 The Ethical Implications of Psychological Manipulation

The manipulation of human behaviour through psychological techniques on social media raises numerous ethical questions. While platforms and advertisers may argue that they are simply offering personalised experiences, the reality is that many of these tactics exploit vulnerabilities in human psychology.

- **Manipulation vs. Persuasion**: The line between persuasion and manipulation is thin. While persuasion involves convincing someone to adopt a belief or take action based on reason or logic, manipulation involves influencing behaviour in a way that bypasses conscious thought, often without the user's awareness or consent.

- **Mental Health Consequences**: The constant exposure to emotionally manipulative content can have lasting effects on mental health, contributing to anxiety, depression, and addiction. Users may not realise the extent to which their behaviour is being shaped by these psychological techniques.

- **Informed Consent**: One of the biggest ethical concerns is the lack of informed consent. Most users are unaware of the psychological techniques being used to influence their behaviour, and platforms are often opaque about how they design their systems to exploit these mechanisms.

4.8 Conclusion

Social media platforms and advertisers have mastered the art of exploiting human psychology to increase engagement, drive behaviour, and generate profit. By leveraging techniques such as dopamine-driven feedback loops, emotional manipulation, and social validation, these platforms keep users hooked and influence their decisions in ways that often go unnoticed.

As we continue to use social media, it is crucial to be aware of the psychological mechanisms at play and to critically evaluate how our behaviours and emotions are being manipulated for profit.

In the next chapter, **Chapter 5: Dark Patterns: Deceptive Design in Social Media Interfaces**, we will explore the subtle and often deceptive design choices used by social media platforms to manipulate user behaviour, such as infinite scrolling, auto-play features, and intentionally confusing settings.

Chapter 5: Dark Patterns: Deceptive Design in Social Media Interfaces

5.1 Introduction: The Hidden Manipulation of Design

While the algorithms and psychological principles that shape our social media experiences often receive attention, the design choices embedded in the very interfaces we interact with are equally powerful tools of manipulation. These design elements, often referred to as **dark patterns**, are intentionally created to guide users toward certain actions that may not necessarily be in their best interest but benefit the platform. Whether through infinite scrolling, auto-play, or confusing privacy settings, these patterns subtly but significantly influence how we use social media.

In this chapter, we will explore the most common dark patterns in social media, dissect how they manipulate user behaviour, and examine the ethical questions surrounding their use.

5.2 Infinite Scrolling: The Trap of Endless Engagement

One of the most pervasive dark patterns in social media is **infinite scrolling**, a feature that automatically loads more content as a user reaches the end of their feed, eliminating the need to manually refresh the page or click through pages. While this may seem like a user-friendly design, its true purpose is to keep users engaged for longer periods of time by removing any natural stopping points.

5.2.1 The Psychological Impact of Infinite Scrolling

Infinite scrolling works by capitalising on the brain's natural desire for **novelty**. Each new piece of content that appears on the screen offers the possibility of something interesting, engaging, or rewarding. The constant flow of new content creates a sense of anticipation, making it difficult for users to stop scrolling.

- **Lack of Stopping Cues**: Traditional media, such as books or newspapers, have natural stopping points—chapters, sections, or page turns—that give the user a sense of closure. Infinite scrolling eliminates these cues, leading to **time distortion** where users underestimate how long they've been engaged with the content.

- **The Zeigarnik Effect**: This psychological principle suggests that people are more likely to remember incomplete tasks than completed ones. Infinite scrolling exploits this by creating an endless task—there's always more content to see, so the user feels compelled to continue.

5.2.2 The Negative Consequences of Infinite Scrolling

While infinite scrolling can increase user engagement, it can also lead to unintended negative consequences. **Prolonged use** of social media without natural breaks can contribute to **social media addiction**, **reduced productivity**, and **mental fatigue**. Users often spend more time than intended on platforms, leading to feelings of regret or frustration.

5.3 Auto-Play: Keeping You Hooked Without Consent

Another common dark pattern in social media is **auto-play**, a feature where videos or audio content automatically start playing as soon as they appear on the user's screen. While auto-play is often marketed as a convenience feature, its primary goal is to keep users engaged without them actively choosing to consume the content.

5.3.1 The Psychology of Passive Consumption

Auto-play capitalises on **passive consumption**, where users continue to watch content without making an active decision to do so. By removing the need for users to click or choose to watch the next video, platforms keep them engaged without giving them time to consciously decide whether they want to continue.

- **Reduced Friction**: Social media platforms intentionally design their interfaces to reduce **friction**, or the small moments when users might stop to think about their actions. Auto-play eliminates friction by seamlessly delivering more content, making it harder for users to disengage.

- **The Role of Visual and Auditory Triggers**: Auto-play also takes advantage of **visual and auditory triggers**. The moment a new video begins to play, the sudden motion and sound capture the user's attention, drawing them back into the platform even if they were about to leave.

5.3.2 Auto-Play and Mental Health

While auto-play can increase user engagement, it can also have a negative impact on mental health. The feature encourages users to spend more time consuming often mindless or irrelevant content, contributing to **decision fatigue** and **information overload**. Additionally, for users who struggle with self-control or time management, auto-play can lead to feelings of guilt or frustration after spending too much time on the platform.

5.4 Intentionally Confusing Settings: The Illusion of Control

Social media platforms often give users the impression that they have control over their privacy settings, notifications, and data usage. However, many of these options are intentionally designed to be confusing or difficult to navigate, leading users to make decisions that benefit the platform rather than themselves.

5.4.1 Obscuring Privacy and Data Settings

One of the most common dark patterns in social media is the deliberate obfuscation of privacy settings. While platforms may claim to offer users control over how their data is collected and shared, the reality is that these settings are often buried in complex menus, written in confusing legal language, or designed to be difficult to change.

- **Default Settings**: Platforms often set default options in ways that maximise data collection, assuming users will not take the time to change them. This tactic is known as **privacy by default**—users are opted into data-sharing practices unless they actively opt out.

- **Choice Overload**: When users do attempt to change their settings, they are often overwhelmed with too many choices, making it difficult to understand what each option means. This leads to **choice overload**, where users are more likely to give up or stick with the default settings.

5.4.2 Consent Fatigue: Exploiting User Apathy

Another tactic used by social media platforms is to bombard users with multiple consent requests, often in the form of pop-ups, notifications, or emails. This can lead to **consent fatigue**, where users become desensitised to these requests and blindly accept terms without fully understanding them.

- **Pre-Checked Boxes**: Many platforms use **pre-checked boxes** for consent to data collection or marketing communications, which users must actively uncheck if they do not want to participate. This design choice manipulates users into agreeing to terms by default.

- **Dark UX**: Dark **user experience (UX)** techniques are used to guide users into making choices that benefit the platform, often without the user realising they've been manipulated. For example, placing a "Continue" button in a prominent position while making the "Opt Out" option less visible.

5.5 Time-Wasting Features: Engaging Users Through Deceptive Design

Some dark patterns are more subtle, such as features designed to **waste users' time** by making it harder for them to navigate away from the platform. These tactics include features like **endless notifications**, **compulsive rewards**, and **confusing exit paths**.

5.5.1 Reward Systems and Gamification

Social media platforms often implement **reward systems** that gamify the user experience, offering badges, achievements, or milestones that encourage users to engage more frequently or stay on the platform longer. While these features may seem harmless, they manipulate users by triggering a sense of **accomplishment** and **social status**.

- **Badges and Achievements**: Platforms like Instagram or TikTok use features like **achievement badges** to reward users for milestones, such as reaching a certain number of followers or likes. This taps into the user's desire for social validation and encourages further engagement.

Another deceptive design technique involves making it difficult for users to log out or disable notifications. Social media platforms often hide these options deep within settings menus or use misleading language to confuse users.

- **Misleading Wording**: Platforms may use confusing language when presenting users with choices, such as "Not Now" instead of "No" or offering ambiguous buttons for important actions like deleting an account or unsubscribing from a service.

- **Exit Obstacles**: Platforms may also introduce unnecessary steps when users attempt to deactivate their accounts or turn off notifications. For example, when users try to delete an account, they may be required to navigate through several screens or input additional information, increasing the likelihood that they will give up before completing the process.

5.6 Ethical Implications of Dark Patterns

The use of dark patterns raises significant ethical concerns about user autonomy, informed consent, and the responsibility of social media platforms to protect users from manipulative practices.

5.6.1 The Balance Between Profit and Ethics

Many social media platforms justify their use of dark patterns as a necessary trade-off between **user engagement** and **profitability**. However, this raises important questions about whether it is ethical to manipulate users in ways that benefit the platform at the expense of their time, privacy, and mental health.

5.6.2 Informed Consent and User Awareness

One of the biggest ethical issues with dark patterns is the lack of **informed consent**. Users are often unaware that they are being manipulated through design choices, and platforms do little to educate users about the potential risks. This creates a power imbalance where platforms hold all the information, while users are left to navigate a system that is designed to confuse and mislead.

5.7 Conclusion

Dark patterns are a subtle but pervasive form of manipulation in social media design. Through features like infinite scrolling, auto-play, and confusing privacy settings, platforms guide users into behaviours that increase engagement and profit, often at the expense of user autonomy and well-being. As users become more aware of these tactics, it is crucial to critically examine how social media interfaces are designed and to demand greater transparency and ethical responsibility from platforms.

In the next chapter, **Chapter 6: Influencers and Manipulation: The Power of Social Proof,** we will explore the role of influencers in manipulating user behaviour through social proof, examining how these figures create trust, shape opinions, and drive purchasing decisions on social media.

Chapter 6: Influencers and Manipulation: The Power of Social Proof

6.1 Introduction: The Rise of the Influencer Economy

In today's digital landscape, **influencers** have become some of the most powerful players in shaping consumer behaviour, trends, and even cultural norms. These individuals, who often amass large followings on platforms such as Instagram, YouTube, and TikTok, wield significant influence over their audiences by promoting products, ideas, and lifestyles. The key to their power lies in **social proof** - the psychological phenomenon where people look to the actions of others to determine appropriate behaviour in uncertain situations.

In this chapter, we will explore the manipulative aspects of social proof used by influencers, how they build trust, shape opinions, and drive purchasing decisions, often blurring the lines between genuine recommendation and profit-driven endorsements.

6.2 The Concept of Social Proof: Why We Follow Influencers

Social proof is a powerful cognitive bias that drives much of our behaviour, particularly in the context of social media. When we are unsure about how to act, what to buy, or what opinions to hold, we often look to others - especially those we trust or admire - for cues. Influencers, by virtue of their large followings and perceived expertise, become trusted sources of validation.

6.2.1 Authority and Expertise

Influencers are often seen as **authorities** in their niche areas - whether it's beauty, fitness, tech, or fashion - making them trusted sources for advice and recommendations. Followers perceive influencers as having **insider knowledge** and expertise, leading them to mimic their behaviour and choices.

- **The Halo Effect**: When influencers are seen as knowledgeable or successful in one area, this perception often extends to other areas, leading followers to trust their opinions on a wide range of topics, even if the influencer is not an expert in those areas.

6.2.2 The Bandwagon Effect

The more followers an influencer has, the more likely it is that new users will trust and follow them. This is known as the **bandwagon effect**, where people assume that if so many others are engaging with and trusting an influencer, they should too.

- **Follower Metrics**: Platforms like Instagram and YouTube prominently display the number of followers, likes, and shares that an influencer has. These metrics act as **social proof** that the influencer is credible and worth following, encouraging users to join the crowd.

6.2.3 Social Identity and FOMO (Fear of Missing Out)

Influencers often cultivate a sense of **community** around their brand, encouraging followers to feel like they are part of a special, exclusive group. This taps into the desire for **social identity**, where individuals align themselves with groups or communities that reflect their values, aspirations, or interests.

- **FOMO**: Influencers often create a sense of **urgency** or **scarcity** around their recommendations, making followers feel like they might miss out on something valuable if they don't act quickly. This can lead to impulsive purchasing decisions or social behaviour driven by fear of being left out.

6.3 Building Trust: The Authenticity Illusion

The power of influencers lies in their ability to create an appearance of **authenticity** and **relatability**, making followers believe they are receiving genuine, unbiased recommendations. However, many influencers are paid or incentivised to promote certain products or services, raising ethical concerns about transparency.

6.3.1 Relatability as a Marketing Tool

Unlike traditional celebrities, influencers often gain their following by presenting themselves as **ordinary people** -someone their audience can relate to. This sense of relatability fosters trust and makes their recommendations feel more personal and genuine.

- **Parasocial Relationships**: Followers often develop **parasocial relationships** with influencers, feeling like they know them personally, even though the relationship is one-sided. This emotional connection makes it easier for influencers to persuade their followers to adopt their viewpoints or make purchases.

6.3.2 Sponsored Content: Blurring the Lines Between Authenticity and Advertising

One of the most manipulative aspects of influencer marketing is the use of **sponsored content**, where influencers are paid to promote products or services, but the advertising is often presented in a way that blurs the line between personal recommendation and paid endorsement.

- **Disguised Promotions**: Many influencers integrate product promotions into their content in subtle ways, making it difficult for followers to distinguish between genuine recommendations and paid advertisements. While regulations require influencers to disclose sponsored content, these disclosures are often not prominent or clear.

- **Trust Exploitation**: The trust influencers build with their audience is often exploited by brands to sell products. Followers may not realise they are being manipulated into purchasing something because the recommendation comes from someone they perceive as trustworthy and authentic.

6.4 Opinion Shaping: The Influence on Beliefs and Values

Influencers do more than just sell products; they also have a significant impact on shaping the **opinions, values, and beliefs** of their followers. This influence can extend to political views, social issues, lifestyle choices, and more, making influencers powerful agents of social change - or manipulation.

6.4.1 Influencers and Social Movements

Influencers have the ability to **amplify social movements** by using their platforms to raise awareness about important causes. However, this can also be a form of manipulation, as influencers may engage with social issues purely for **self-promotion** or **brand alignment**, rather than genuine activism.

- **Virtue Signalling**: Some influencers engage in **virtue signalling**, where they promote social causes or political movements to appear morally superior or to gain social capital, without making meaningful contributions to the cause.

6.4.2 Creating Norms and Expectations

Influencers set trends and create norms around **beauty standards, lifestyle choices**, and **consumer behaviour**. This can manipulate followers into adopting certain behaviours or beliefs to fit in with what is perceived as popular or acceptable in the digital world.

- **Body Image and Self-Esteem**: Influencers who promote unattainable beauty standards can manipulate followers into feeling inadequate, driving them to purchase products, engage in extreme diets, or undergo cosmetic procedures in order to meet these standards.

6.5 Driving Consumer Behaviour: The Business of Influence

At its core, the influencer economy is about driving **consumer behaviour**. Influencers are often used as marketing tools by brands to generate sales, and their power to influence purchasing decisions is a direct result of the social proof they provide.

6.5.1 The Impact of Affiliate Marketing

Many influencers participate in **affiliate marketing**, where they earn a commission for every sale made through a link they provide. While this can be a legitimate business model, it also raises ethical concerns, as influencers may prioritise promoting products that earn them a higher commission over those that genuinely benefit their followers.

- **Hidden Incentives**: Followers are often unaware of the financial incentives driving influencer recommendations, making it easier for influencers to manipulate their audience into making purchases.

6.5.2 The Role of Giveaways and Contests

Influencers often use **giveaways** and **contests** to increase engagement and followers. While these tactics can seem like harmless promotions, they are often used to manipulate users into performing certain actions - such as sharing content, following accounts, or engaging with posts - under the guise of receiving a reward.

- **Engagement Manipulation**: By promising followers the chance to win a prize, influencers can artificially inflate their engagement metrics, making them appear more popular and credible, thereby increasing their social proof.

6.6 Ethical Implications of Influencer Manipulation

The manipulative practices of influencers raise important ethical questions about **transparency, accountability**, and the impact of social proof on consumer behaviour. While influencers provide value by sharing their experiences and expertise, the blurred line between genuine recommendation and paid promotion makes it difficult for followers to make informed decisions.

6.6.1 Transparency in Sponsored Content

One of the primary ethical concerns in influencer marketing is the lack of transparency around **sponsored content**. While regulations exist to ensure influencers disclose paid partnerships, the enforcement of these rules is inconsistent, leading to followers being misled.

- **The Need for Clear Disclosures**: Influencers should be required to clearly and prominently disclose when they are being paid to promote a product or service, so followers can make informed choices about the content they consume.

6.6.2 The Responsibility of Platforms and Brands

Social media platforms and brands that collaborate with influencers also bear responsibility for ensuring that their marketing practices are ethical. This includes enforcing transparency, preventing manipulative tactics, and protecting users from deceptive advertising.

6.7 Conclusion

Influencers have become a central part of the social media ecosystem, wielding the power of social proof to shape opinions, drive consumer behaviour, and influence cultural norms. While their ability to connect with audiences offers many benefits, it also opens the door to manipulation. As influencers continue to play a significant role in our digital lives, it is crucial to recognise the tactics they use and to approach their content with a critical eye.

In the next chapter, **Chapter 7: The Science of Virality: How Content Goes Viral**, we will explore the strategies used by social media platforms and influencers to make content go viral, examining the psychological triggers and design features that drive mass engagement.

Chapter 7: The Science of Virality: How Content Goes Viral

7.1 Introduction: The Allure of Going Viral

In the digital age, **going viral** has become a coveted goal for influencers, brands, and everyday users alike. Viral content—whether it's a video, meme, or social media post—has the potential to reach millions in a matter of hours, dramatically amplifying the message, brand, or person behind it. But what makes some content explode in popularity while other content fades into obscurity?

In this chapter, we will explore the **science of virality**—the combination of psychological triggers, algorithmic strategies, and design features that make content go viral. We'll break down how platforms and influencers exploit these elements to maximise engagement and achieve widespread reach.

7.2 The Psychological Triggers Behind Viral Content

At the core of virality lies human **psychology**. Content that triggers strong emotional reactions, appeals to our desire for social connection, or taps into our need for novelty is more likely to be shared widely.

7.2.1 Emotionally Charged Content

Content that evokes **strong emotions** - whether positive or negative - is more likely to be shared and engaged with. Emotions such as **joy, surprise, anger**, or **fear** trigger heightened psychological states that prompt people to act, either by sharing the content, commenting, or liking it.

- **Positive Emotions**: Content that makes people feel good, such as heartwarming stories or funny videos, tends to spread quickly. These types of posts foster feelings of **happiness, awe**, or **amusement**, making them more shareable.

- **Negative Emotions**: Anger, outrage, or fear can also fuel virality. Content that sparks **controversy** or highlights a problem often gets shared because people feel compelled to spread awareness or express their opinions.

7.2.2 Social Validation and Identity

People are more likely to share content that reflects their **values, beliefs**, or sense of identity. Sharing content becomes a form of **self-expression**, allowing individuals to signal their membership in certain social groups or communicate their worldview to others.

- **Virtue Signalling**: Users often share content to appear morally or socially aware. For example, posts related to social justice movements, environmental issues, or charitable causes are shared widely, in part, because they allow people to showcase their **virtue** and alignment with social values.

- **Memes and In-Group Culture**: Memes, jokes, and slang that reflect **in-group culture** or specific subcultures often go viral within certain communities. These pieces of content serve as markers of identity and belonging, making them highly shareable within tight-knit social groups.

7.2.3 Novelty and Surprise

Humans are hardwired to notice and share things that are **novel** or **unexpected**. Content that presents something surprising, new, or out of the ordinary stands out in the crowded landscape of social media, making it more likely to catch attention and be shared.

- **Shock Factor**: Content that surprises or shocks the viewer can rapidly go viral due to its novelty. This is often seen in viral challenges, pranks, or unexpected plot twists in videos.

- **Curiosity Gap**: Headlines or teasers that create a **curiosity gap**—where users are intrigued by what they don't know—drive people to click, engage, and share. The promise of surprising or unexpected information encourages users to share content before even fully engaging with it.

7.3 The Role of Algorithms in Amplifying Virality

While human psychology plays a crucial role in what content goes viral, social media **algorithms** act as the engine that powers its rapid spread. These algorithms prioritise content that drives engagement, keeping users on the platform longer and generating more revenue through ads.

7.3.1 Engagement Maximisation

Social media platforms like Facebook, Instagram, and TikTok use algorithms designed to maximise **engagement** by pushing content that receives high levels of interaction. Content that attracts a large number of likes, comments, shares, and views is pushed to more users, creating a **positive feedback loop** that amplifies its reach.

- **Content That Drives Interaction**: Posts that prompt **comments**, such as controversial opinions or discussion-starting questions, are more likely to go viral because they increase engagement. Similarly, content that encourages users to **tag friends** or respond also fuels the algorithm's engagement metrics.

- **The Snowball Effect**: Once a post starts gaining traction, algorithms amplify its reach by showing it to more users, leading to further engagement and creating a **snowball effect**. This momentum is critical to virality.

7.3.2 Timing and Trends

Algorithms also favour content that taps into **current trends** or is posted at times when users are most active. Influencers and brands exploit this by timing their posts around peak user activity or by piggybacking on viral trends to increase the likelihood of their content being shared.

- **Trend Hijacking**: Tapping into existing viral trends, challenges, or hashtags allows content to be seen by a wider audience already interested in the topic. This strategy is often used by influencers to insert themselves into the viral conversation and increase their visibility.

- **Peak Posting Times**: Content posted during high-traffic times is more likely to be seen, liked, and shared. Platforms like Instagram and Twitter have peak hours for engagement, and content creators use analytics to optimise the timing of their posts for maximum exposure.

7.3.3 Virality Through Platform Design

Social media platforms are designed with specific features that encourage viral sharing. These design elements, often referred to as **virality hacks**, nudge users to spread content quickly and widely.

- **Share Buttons**: Easy access to share buttons encourages users to repost content with minimal effort, increasing its reach.

- **Notifications**: Platforms often send users notifications when their content is shared or liked, encouraging them to engage further and promote it.

- **Video Autoplay**: The autoplay feature used by platforms like TikTok and Facebook increases video views by automatically playing content as users scroll through their feeds, boosting the visibility of videos and making them more likely to go viral.

7.4 The Role of Influencers in Virality

Influencers are a crucial factor in making content go viral. By sharing content with their large followings, they can rapidly amplify its reach. In some cases, a single influencer sharing a piece of content can trigger a **viral cascade**, leading to mass exposure.

7.4.1 The Power of Influencer Endorsement

When an influencer shares or endorses content, it lends **credibility** and **social proof** to the post, making it more appealing to their followers. Followers are more likely to engage with content shared by someone they trust or admire, increasing the likelihood of it going viral.

- **Micro-Influencers**: While mega-influencers with millions of followers have obvious reach, **micro-influencers**—those with smaller, more engaged followings—can also drive virality within niche communities. Their content feels more authentic and relatable, making it more likely to be shared within specific subcultures.

- **Collaborations**: Influencers often collaborate with each other, cross-promoting content to their combined followings, effectively doubling or tripling the potential for virality.

Influencers frequently use **call-to-action (CTA)** strategies to encourage their followers to share, comment, or engage with content, which boosts its chances of going viral. This could be as simple as asking followers to "tag a friend" or participate in a viral challenge.

- **Challenges and Contests**: Viral challenges, where influencers encourage followers to recreate content or participate in a trend, are a powerful tool for spreading content. These challenges create a **chain reaction** where each participant generates new content, further amplifying the original post.

7.5 Dark Side of Virality: Manipulation and Misinformation

While virality can be a force for good, spreading important messages or bringing attention to worthy causes, it can also be used to spread **misinformation**, **manipulate opinions**, and create **toxic environments**.

7.5.1 Misinformation and Fake News

Viral content is often created or shared without fact-checking, leading to the rapid spread of **misinformation**. This can have serious consequences, from influencing elections to damaging reputations, as false information spreads more quickly than corrections.

- **Emotional Manipulation**: Misinformation often goes viral because it taps into **emotional triggers** such as fear, anger, or outrage. These emotions make people more likely to share content without verifying its accuracy.

7.5.2 Amplification of Harmful Content

Algorithms prioritise content that generates strong emotional reactions, which can lead to the **amplification of harmful or divisive content**. Toxic discussions, hate speech, and harmful challenges often go viral because they provoke strong reactions from users, which drives engagement.

7.6 Conclusion

The science of virality is a complex interplay between **psychological triggers**, **algorithmic design**, and **influencer amplification**. While viral content can entertain, inform, and connect people, it also has the potential to manipulate and misinform. As social media continues to shape our digital landscape, understanding the factors that drive virality is crucial for navigating this fast-paced and often unpredictable world.

In the next chapter, **Chapter 8: The Role of Emotion in Social Media Manipulation**, we will explore how emotional manipulation is used on social media platforms to keep users engaged, examining the specific tactics used to trigger emotional responses and influence behaviour.

Chapter 8: The Role of Emotion in Social Media Manipulation

8.1 Introduction: Emotional Manipulation as a Tool of Engagement

In the attention economy, where social media platforms compete for users' time and focus, **emotional engagement** has become a critical tool. The more intensely a user feels—whether joy, anger, or fear—the more likely they are to remain engaged, interact with content, and return to the platform. Emotions are a powerful driver of human behaviour, and social media platforms have become experts at leveraging emotional manipulation to keep users hooked.

In this chapter, we will explore how emotional manipulation is used in social media design and content strategies, examining specific tactics that trigger emotional responses and influence user behaviour. We will also consider the ethical implications of these tactics and the impact they have on individual well-being and social discourse.

8.2 Emotional Triggers: The Science of Engagement

Human emotions are deeply tied to our decision-making processes and behaviour. Social media platforms and content creators tap into this understanding by designing content and features that provoke strong emotional reactions. Emotional content tends to elicit more likes, shares, and comments, which are the primary metrics of success for social media platforms.

8.2.1 The Role of Dopamine in User Behaviour

At the heart of emotional manipulation on social media is the brain's **dopamine system**. Dopamine is a neurotransmitter associated with pleasure and reward. Social media platforms are designed to create **dopamine-driven feedback loops**, where users receive intermittent rewards—such as likes, comments, or shares—that trigger small bursts of dopamine, encouraging them to engage more.

- **Variable Rewards**: Like slot machines, social media platforms deliver rewards at unpredictable intervals. Users may not know when they will receive a like or comment, but the possibility keeps them returning to the platform in search of that dopamine hit.

- **The Power of Notifications**: Notifications, whether for a new message, a like, or a comment, serve as triggers for these dopamine responses. The anticipation of social validation makes users more likely to check their phones repeatedly, creating habitual use.

8.2.2 Emotional Valence: Positive vs. Negative Content

Both **positive** and **negative** emotions can drive engagement, but they do so in different ways. Content that makes people feel good—such as uplifting stories, humour, or beautiful images—encourages users to share it to spread joy. However, negative emotions like **anger, fear**, and **outrage** often drive more intense and immediate reactions.

- **Positive Content**: Content that evokes **happiness, awe**, or **inspiration** tends to be highly shareable because it reinforces social bonds and fosters a sense of community. Memes, cute animal videos, and motivational posts are examples of emotionally positive content that performs well.

- **Negative Content**: While positive content may build communities, negative content often spreads faster and provokes more intense engagement. Posts that evoke **outrage** or **fear**—such as political controversies, scandals, or divisive news—are highly shareable because they spark strong emotional responses, leading to comments, debates, and shares.

8.2.3 Emotional Contagion: Spreading Emotions Through Networks

On social media, emotions are **contagious**. Studies have shown that seeing emotional content in a user's feed can influence their own emotional state, leading them to share similarly emotional content. This is especially true for **negative emotions**, which tend to spread more rapidly and widely than positive ones.

- **Amplification of Anger**: Social media platforms often amplify anger and outrage because these emotions drive high engagement. When users see posts that provoke anger, they are more likely to respond with comments, shares, or retweets, further amplifying the reach of the content.

- **Echo Chambers**: Social media algorithms often create **echo chambers** where users are primarily exposed to content that reinforces their existing beliefs and emotions. This can lead to the amplification of emotionally charged content, particularly when it aligns with the user's worldview.

8.3 Tactics for Emotional Manipulation on Social Media

Social media platforms and content creators employ a variety of **tactics** to manipulate users' emotions, keeping them engaged and encouraging them to interact with content. These tactics can be subtle or overt, but all are designed to trigger emotional responses and increase time spent on the platform.

8.3.1 Fear and Scarcity: The Power of FOMO

One of the most common emotional manipulation tactics on social media is the use of **fear of missing out (FOMO)**. Social media platforms are designed to create a sense of urgency, making users feel that if they don't constantly check in, they will miss out on important news, trends, or social interactions.

- **Limited-Time Content**: Features like **Stories** on Instagram and Facebook, which disappear after 24 hours, create a sense of urgency and encourage users to check the app more frequently to avoid missing out.

- **Push Notifications**: Push notifications often exploit FOMO by alerting users to new messages, trending content, or likes on their posts. The fear of missing out on social interactions or validation drives users to engage more frequently.

8.3.2 Outrage and Polarisation

Outrage is a particularly potent tool for emotional manipulation. Content that sparks anger or frustration tends to go viral quickly because it elicits strong emotional responses and encourages users to engage in debates or arguments.

- **Outrage Content**: Posts that provoke anger - whether by highlighting social injustices, political controversies, or scandals - are shared widely because users feel compelled to express their outrage. This drives high engagement and increases the reach of the content.

- **Polarising Discussions**: Platforms often promote polarising content because it generates more comments, shares, and time spent on the platform. By presenting users with content that aligns with their views and simultaneously exposing them to opposing opinions, platforms fuel emotional debates that keep users engaged.

8.3.3 Social Validation and Peer Pressure

Social validation is a powerful motivator for emotional engagement. Social media platforms exploit users' desire for **likes, comments**, and **shares**—forms of social validation that make users feel valued and connected to their peers.

- **Like and Comment Systems**: The design of like buttons and comment sections taps into users' need for social approval. Posts that receive more likes and comments are prioritised by algorithms, creating a feedback loop where users feel compelled to post content that will be validated by their peers.

- **Tagging and Mentions**: Platforms encourage users to tag friends in posts, which creates a chain of social validation. When users are tagged in a post, they are more likely to engage with it, driving further interaction and extending the post's reach.

8.3.4 Emotional Headlines and Clickbait

Another common tactic is the use of **emotional headlines** and **clickbait** to draw users in. These headlines often exaggerate or sensationalise content to provoke emotional responses, enticing users to click and engage.

- **Sensationalism**: Emotional headlines that promise shocking or unbelievable content (e.g., "You won't believe what happened next!") exploit users' curiosity and emotional reactions to drive clicks and shares.

- **Manipulative Language**: Phrases like "This will make you angry" or "Prepare to be amazed" are designed to evoke emotional responses before the user even views the content, setting the stage for emotional engagement.

8.4 The Ethical Debate: Is Emotional Manipulation Justifiable?

The use of emotional manipulation on social media raises important **ethical questions**. On one hand, emotional engagement is key to the success of social media platforms and can be used to spread positive messages, foster community, and raise awareness about important causes. On the other hand, the deliberate exploitation of emotions for profit - often without users' awareness - poses significant risks to mental health and social cohesion.

8.4.1 Mental Health Impacts

Constant exposure to emotionally charged content, particularly negative emotions like anger and fear, can take a toll on users' mental health. Studies have shown that prolonged use of social media can lead to increased **anxiety, depression**, and feelings of isolation, particularly when users are exposed to high levels of negative emotional content.

- **Doomscrolling**: The habit of endlessly scrolling through negative news and posts, often referred to as "doomscrolling," can exacerbate stress and anxiety. Social media platforms, by design, promote this behaviour by continually serving emotionally charged content.

8.4.2 Manipulation of Free Will

Another ethical concern is the **manipulation of free will**. Social media platforms and content creators use emotional manipulation to influence users' behaviour, often in ways that users are unaware of. This raises questions about whether users are truly making free choices or if their behaviour is being subtly manipulated by algorithms designed to exploit their emotions.

8.5 Conclusion: Navigating Emotional Manipulation in the Digital Age

Emotional manipulation is a powerful tool used by social media platforms to keep users engaged and drive interaction. While it can be used to build connections and spread positive messages, it can also lead to the spread of misinformation, polarisation, and negative mental health impacts. Understanding how these tactics work is the first step toward navigating social media more mindfully and regaining control over emotional responses in the digital age.

In the next chapter, **Chapter 9: Misinformation and Fake News: Manipulating Public Perception**, we will explore how misinformation spreads on social media, examining the role of algorithms, emotional manipulation, and platform design in shaping public perception.

Chapter 9: Misinformation and Fake News: Manipulating Public Perception

9.1 Introduction: The Rise of Misinformation in the Digital Age

In the age of social media, the rapid spread of **misinformation** and **fake news** has become one of the most pressing challenges for online platforms and society as a whole. Social media has accelerated the dissemination of false or misleading information, often blurring the lines between fact and fiction. This chapter will explore how misinformation spreads across social platforms, how algorithms amplify it, and how emotional manipulation and platform design contribute to shaping public perception.

9.2 The Anatomy of Misinformation: What is Fake News?

Fake news refers to **deliberately false or misleading information** presented as legitimate news. While misinformation can spread unintentionally due to misunderstandings or errors, fake news is often crafted with the intention of **manipulating public opinion**, influencing political outcomes, or generating profit through clicks and shares.

- **Clickbait**: Sensational or misleading headlines designed to attract clicks, often using exaggerated claims.

- **Satirical Content**: News satire that is often misinterpreted as factual, despite its humorous or exaggerated nature.

- **Deepfakes**: Manipulated media, including videos and images, designed to deceive viewers into believing something false.

- **Conspiracy Theories**: Content promoting unsubstantiated claims or alternative narratives, often targeting emotionally vulnerable audiences.

- **Pseudo-Science**: Content that presents unproven or debunked theories as factual science, misleading users on health, climate change, or other critical issues.

9.3 How Algorithms Amplify Misinformation

Algorithms play a crucial role in determining what content users see on social media. These algorithms are primarily designed to **increase engagement**, showing users content that is most likely to spark interaction - whether that content is factual or not.

9.3.1 The Filter Bubble Effect

One of the key ways algorithms spread misinformation is by creating **filter bubbles**. Filter bubbles occur when algorithms tailor content to fit users' existing beliefs and preferences, effectively isolating them from opposing viewpoints. This can lead to an **echo chamber** effect, where users are repeatedly exposed to the same types of misinformation, reinforcing false beliefs.

- **Personalisation of Content**: Social media platforms use data about users' interests, past interactions, and behaviours to personalise their news feed. While this can make the user experience more relevant, it also means users are likely to encounter content that confirms their biases rather than challenges them.

- **Amplification of Outrage**: Algorithms favour emotionally charged content because it drives higher levels of engagement. Posts that provoke anger, fear, or outrage are more likely to be promoted, even if they contain false or misleading information. This is particularly dangerous when it comes to fake news, as misinformation designed to evoke strong emotions spreads faster and more widely than factual content.

Studies have shown that false information spreads **faster and more widely** on social media than the truth. Part of this is due to the emotional nature of much fake news - stories designed to shock, anger, or awe are more likely to go viral. However, the viral spread of misinformation is also driven by the **design of social platforms**, which reward engagement with more visibility.

- **Rapid Sharing Features**: Social media makes it easy for users to share content with just one click. This frictionless sharing means that users can spread misinformation without fully understanding or verifying it.

- **Trending Topics and Hashtags**: Misinformation is often boosted by trending topics or hashtags. Once a piece of fake news starts gaining traction, it can be picked up by algorithms and displayed to a wider audience, even those who wouldn't otherwise have encountered it.

9.4 Emotional Manipulation and Misinformation

Emotions are powerful drivers of user behaviour on social media, and this is particularly true when it comes to the spread of misinformation. Misinformation often relies on **emotional manipulation** to make users more likely to believe and share false content.

9.4.1 Fear, Anger, and Outrage

False information is often crafted to evoke **strong emotional reactions**, particularly fear, anger, and outrage. These emotions tend to override critical thinking, making users more likely to accept and spread misleading content without verifying its accuracy.

- **Fear-Based Misinformation**: Health scares, conspiracy theories, and stories about threats (whether real or imagined) often rely on fear to spread. For example, during the COVID-19 pandemic, misinformation about vaccines, treatments, and the virus's origins was heavily driven by fear.

- **Political Outrage**: Political misinformation often taps into anger and outrage to provoke strong responses. This has been especially evident in the context of elections and other politically charged events, where fake news stories are crafted to stoke division and outrage.

9.4.2 Confirmation Bias and Cognitive Dissonance

Misinformation exploits **confirmation bias** - the tendency to believe information that aligns with our pre-existing views while dismissing contradictory information. Social media platforms feed into this by showing users content that aligns with their beliefs, leading them to accept misinformation that confirms their biases without critical examination.

- **Reinforcement of Beliefs**: When users encounter fake news that aligns with their political, religious, or social views, they are more likely to accept it as true. Confirmation bias makes it easier for fake news to take root, especially when it plays into deeply held beliefs or emotional narratives.

- **Cognitive Dissonance**: Users may also experience **cognitive dissonance** when presented with information that contradicts their beliefs. In such cases, they are more likely to reject the accurate information and double down on the misinformation they already believe.

9.5 Platform Design: Features That Enable Misinformation

The design of social media platforms also plays a role in the spread of misinformation. Certain features - while intended to enhance user experience - can be exploited to **manipulate users** and propagate fake news.

9.5.1 Sharing Features and Low Accountability

Social media platforms make sharing content **easy and instantaneous**. While this is intended to facilitate communication and engagement, it also makes it possible for users to spread misinformation with minimal effort or accountability.

- **Frictionless Sharing**: Platforms like Facebook and Twitter allow users to share content with a single click, which reduces the likelihood that users will fact-check or critically evaluate content before sharing it.

- **Anonymous and Fake Accounts**: The anonymity of social media makes it easier for bad actors—such as bots or fake accounts—to spread misinformation without accountability. Many misinformation campaigns are driven by automated accounts that mimic real users.

9.5.2 Recommendation Algorithms and Engagement Loops

Recommendation algorithms, such as the ones used by YouTube or TikTok, often promote sensational or emotionally charged content because it leads to higher engagement. This can result in a **feedback loop** where users are continually shown more extreme or misleading content, reinforcing their beliefs and leading them further down the rabbit hole of misinformation.

- **Auto-Play and Content Suggestions**: On platforms like YouTube, auto-play features and algorithm-driven content suggestions can gradually push users toward more radical or misleading content. For example, someone watching a video about a legitimate political issue may be recommended increasingly conspiratorial or extreme content.

- **Engagement-Driven Recommendations**: Platforms prioritise content that generates likes, shares, and comments, even if that content is misleading or false. This can create a perverse incentive for creators to produce fake news or sensationalised content to maximise engagement and reach.

9.6 The Real-World Impact of Misinformation

The spread of misinformation has significant real-world consequences. Beyond shaping individual beliefs and behaviours, it can influence **elections**, **public health**, and **social stability**.

9.6.1 Political Manipulation and Election Interference

Misinformation has been weaponised to interfere in elections and manipulate political outcomes. During elections, fake news stories designed to discredit candidates, spread false narratives, or inflame divisions can influence voters and skew the results.

- **Foreign Interference**: In some cases, misinformation campaigns are orchestrated by foreign governments seeking to disrupt or influence the political processes of other countries. For example, during the 2016 U.S. presidential election, Russian interference included the spread of misinformation on social media platforms to sow division and influence voter behaviour.

9.6.2 Public Health Crises

Misinformation can have devastating consequences for public health. During health crises such as the COVID-19 pandemic, the spread of fake news about vaccines, treatments, and the virus itself undermined efforts to control the outbreak and led to widespread **vaccine hesitancy**.

- **Health Misinformation**: False claims about the safety and efficacy of vaccines have caused real harm, with many people refusing vaccinations based on misinformation they encountered online. This has had serious consequences for global health efforts.

9.6.3 Social Polarisation

Misinformation can deepen **social polarisation** by reinforcing existing divisions and creating new ones. When users are exposed to fake news that aligns with their beliefs and vilifies opposing views, it can lead to increased **polarisation**, making it harder for people to engage in civil discourse or find common ground.

9.7 Combating Misinformation: Solutions and Challenges

Efforts to combat misinformation are ongoing, but they face significant challenges due to the nature of social media and the design of algorithms. However, there are some strategies that can help mitigate the spread of fake news.

9.7.1 Fact-Checking and Verification

Fact-checking organisations work to verify the accuracy of news stories and content on social media. Platforms like Facebook have also implemented **fact-checking labels** on posts that contain false information, though these measures are not always effective in curbing the spread of misinformation.

9.7.2 Algorithmic Solutions

Some platforms are experimenting with **algorithmic changes** that prioritise high-quality, verified content over sensationalised or misleading content. However, these changes can be difficult to implement without impacting the user experience or engagement metrics.

9.7.3 Media Literacy and User Education

Improving users' **media literacy** is one of the most effective ways to combat misinformation. By teaching users how to critically evaluate content, verify sources, and recognise emotional manipulation, platforms can empower users to make informed decisions about what they believe and share.

9.8 Conclusion: Navigating the Information Landscape

Misinformation and fake news are serious challenges in the digital age, with wide-reaching consequences for society. By understanding the role of algorithms, emotional manipulation, and platform design, users can become more discerning consumers of information and help combat the spread of fake news.

In the next chapter, **Chapter 10: The Dark Web: Myths, Realities, and Manipulation**, we will explore the world of the dark web, dispelling common myths and examining how it is used to manipulate and exploit users in ways that are often hidden from the public eye.

Chapter 10: The Dark Web: Myths, Realities, and Manipulation

10.1 Introduction: Understanding the Dark Web

The **dark web** has long been shrouded in mystery, often portrayed as a shadowy, lawless corner of the internet where illegal activities thrive. While there is some truth to this reputation, much of what the public understands about the dark web is shaped by myths and sensationalised media portrayals. In reality, the dark web is a complex environment where both **illicit activity** and **legitimate use** coexist. This chapter will unpack the myths surrounding the dark web, examine its realities, and explore how it is used to manipulate and exploit users.

10.2 What is the Dark Web?

To understand the dark web, it's essential to distinguish between the **surface web**, **deep web**, and **dark web**. The **surface web** refers to the part of the internet that is indexed by search engines like Google - this includes websites we use every day. The **deep web** is made up of parts of the internet that aren't indexed by search engines but are still accessible, such as private databases or academic resources. The **dark web** is a small part of the deep web that is intentionally hidden and accessible only through special software like **Tor** (The Onion Router).

10.2.1 How the Dark Web Works

The dark web relies on encryption and anonymisation technologies to protect the identities of its users and the locations of websites. Unlike traditional websites, dark web URLs are often long, random strings of characters, ending in **.onion**, which are inaccessible through standard browsers. This anonymity makes the dark web appealing for those seeking privacy, but it also enables **criminal activity**, making it a haven for illegal marketplaces, hackers, and exploitative schemes.

10.3 Myths vs. Realities of the Dark Web

10.3.1 Myth: The Dark Web is Entirely Illegal

A common misconception is that everything on the dark web is illegal. While it is true that the dark web hosts **criminal activity**, it is also used by **whistleblowers**, **journalists**, and **activists** in repressive regimes to communicate and share information without fear of surveillance. **Legitimate use cases** include secure communication channels for human rights organisations, alternative internet access for individuals in censored countries, and private online forums.

10.3.2 Reality: Criminal Networks and Illicit Marketplaces Thrive

Despite some legitimate use, the dark web does host significant **illegal activities**, including the sale of drugs, weapons, stolen data, and illegal services like hacking. **Darknet markets**, such as the infamous **Silk Road**, have gained notoriety for facilitating these activities. These markets are typically organised similarly to e-commerce platforms, with user reviews, escrow services, and digital currencies like **Bitcoin** enabling anonymous transactions.

10.3.3 Myth: The Dark Web is Easy to Access and Use

While accessing the dark web via software like Tor is straightforward, navigating it is not as simple as mainstream media portrays. Websites are not easily discoverable through search engines, and users need to rely on **word of mouth**, **forums**, and **trusted directories** to find specific sites. This complexity acts as a barrier for casual users but also shields illicit communities from unwanted attention.

10.4 How the Dark Web is Used for Manipulation

10.4.1 Identity Theft and Financial Manipulation

One of the most common forms of exploitation on the dark web is **identity theft**. **Personal information**, such as credit card numbers, social security numbers, and login credentials, are bought and sold on the dark web. Criminals use this information to commit **financial fraud**, manipulate bank accounts, and even sell fake identities to others.

10.4.2 Manipulative Services: Hacking and DDoS Attacks

The dark web offers a range of manipulative services, including hiring hackers for **data breaches**, **DDoS (Distributed Denial of Service)** attacks, and cyber-espionage. These services are typically available on specialised forums and marketplaces, often advertised with guarantees of success or anonymity. These capabilities are sometimes used by individuals, criminal organisations, or even governments to target individuals or institutions for manipulation or disruption.

10.4.3 Blackmail and Extortion Schemes

Ransomware and **blackmail** schemes thrive on the dark web. After obtaining sensitive or compromising data, hackers often use the threat of public exposure to extort money from victims. Ransomware attacks typically involve encrypting a victim's data and demanding payment in cryptocurrency for its release. High-profile targets include businesses, celebrities, and politicians, but ordinary individuals are increasingly falling prey to these manipulative schemes as well.

10.5 The Role of Cryptocurrency in Dark Web Transactions

The rise of **cryptocurrency** has made it easier for dark web users to engage in anonymous transactions. **Bitcoin**, the first widely adopted cryptocurrency, became the currency of choice on early darknet marketplaces, though privacy-focused alternatives like **Monero** have since gained popularity due to their enhanced anonymity features. While cryptocurrencies have legitimate uses, they are also favoured by criminals for their relative untraceability, enabling financial manipulation, money laundering, and black-market trade.

10.5.1 The Appeal of Monero

Monero stands out from Bitcoin due to its focus on **privacy and confidentiality**. Unlike Bitcoin transactions, which can be traced through the public blockchain, Monero transactions are designed to be **completely anonymous**. This makes Monero highly appealing for illegal transactions on the dark web, particularly for services that rely on anonymity, such as drug markets, illegal arms sales, or even hitman services.

10.6 Exploiting the Anonymity of the Dark Web

The **anonymity** provided by the dark web offers opportunities for manipulation, both in terms of illegal commerce and information warfare. Criminals exploit this anonymity to engage in illicit trade without revealing their identities, while hackers and cybercriminals leverage the dark web for **covert communication** and **coordination of cyberattacks**.

10.6.1 Coordinating Misinformation and Manipulation Campaigns

Beyond illegal commerce, the dark web has been used by **political actors** and **state-sponsored groups** to coordinate disinformation campaigns, manipulate public perception, and interfere in democratic processes. These activities include the sale of **stolen data**, **voter manipulation**, and **political blackmail**, all conducted behind the veil of anonymity. This makes it difficult to trace the origins of manipulation campaigns, which can have far-reaching consequences for society and governance.

10.6.2 Human Exploitation and Trafficking

One of the darkest realities of the dark web is its role in **human exploitation**. **Human trafficking** networks operate in secrecy on the dark web, where they advertise services ranging from illegal labour to sexual exploitation. The anonymity provided by dark web marketplaces has made it difficult for law enforcement agencies to track down traffickers, creating a significant challenge in combating modern-day slavery and exploitation.

10.7 Law Enforcement on the Dark Web: Challenges and Tactics

Despite the anonymity and privacy of the dark web, law enforcement agencies have made significant efforts to crack down on illegal activities. However, tracking down criminals operating on the dark web presents unique challenges, especially due to the encryption technologies that shield users' identities.

10.7.1 Law Enforcement Infiltration

One common tactic is for law enforcement to **infiltrate** dark web marketplaces, posing as buyers or sellers to gather intelligence on illegal activities. This often involves undercover agents building trust within illicit communities to gather evidence that can lead to arrests. **Operation Bayonet**, for instance, led to the takedown of AlphaBay, one of the largest dark web marketplaces, through a coordinated law enforcement effort.

10.7.2 Seizing Control of Dark Web Platforms

Another law enforcement strategy involves **seizing control** of dark web sites or markets and shutting them down. However, these shutdowns are often temporary, as new sites typically spring up to replace those that were taken offline. In some cases, law enforcement agencies have used seized dark web platforms to gather information on users, leading to further arrests and crackdowns.

10.7.3 The Role of Technology in Law Enforcement

Law enforcement agencies increasingly rely on sophisticated technologies, such as **blockchain analysis**, to trace cryptocurrency transactions and identify users engaging in illicit trade. By following the digital trail left by transactions, authorities can connect seemingly anonymous activities to real-world identities.

10.8 Conclusion: Navigating the Myths and Realities of the Dark Web

The dark web is a complex and multifaceted environment that offers both legitimate and illegal use cases. While it provides a haven for **privacy** and **free speech** in repressive environments, it also facilitates some of the most exploitative and manipulative activities on the internet. Understanding the realities behind the myths of the dark web is crucial to navigating its dangers and addressing the challenges it presents for both users and society as a whole.

In the next chapter, **Chapter 11: Manipulating Perception: The Role of Social Media in Shaping Reality**, we will explore how social media platforms manipulate user perception by shaping the content they see and influencing how they understand the world around them.

Chapter 11: Manipulating Perception: The Role of Social Media in Shaping Reality

11.1 Introduction: Shaping Our Reality Through Social Media

Social media has become a powerful force in shaping how we perceive the world around us. From the news we consume to the way we interact with others, social platforms significantly influence our understanding of reality. **Algorithms**, **echo chambers**, and **content curation** play pivotal roles in filtering the information we see, making social media a potent tool for manipulating our perceptions. In this chapter, we will explore the mechanisms through which social media shapes our understanding of the world and examine how this power can be exploited for manipulative purposes.

11.2 Filter Bubbles and Echo Chambers: Limiting Our Worldview

11.2.1 What are Filter Bubbles?

Filter bubbles refer to the algorithmic filtering of content on social media that shows users information they are most likely to engage with, based on their past behaviour. While this creates a personalised experience, it also limits exposure to diverse perspectives and reinforces pre-existing beliefs. Filter bubbles can lead to a distorted understanding of reality, where users are only presented with information that aligns with their views.

11.2.2 Echo Chambers: Reinforcing Beliefs

Closely related to filter bubbles, **echo chambers** occur when users surround themselves with like-minded individuals, either by following specific influencers or joining groups that share similar beliefs. In echo chambers, dissenting viewpoints are often excluded or minimised, which amplifies certain perspectives while suppressing others. This environment reinforces users' existing beliefs, making it difficult for them to critically evaluate new or opposing information.

11.2.3 The Danger of Polarisation

The combination of filter bubbles and echo chambers can exacerbate **polarisation** within society. When users are exposed only to content that aligns with their views, they are less likely to engage with differing opinions, creating a sense of "us versus them." This can lead to increased political and ideological divides, as well as the spread of **extreme views**.

11.3 Algorithms as Gatekeepers of Information

11.3.1 How Algorithms Curate Content

Social media algorithms are designed to maximise user engagement by curating the content that appears in users' feeds. These algorithms prioritise posts, advertisements, and news stories based on factors such as **user preferences**, **engagement history**, and **content virality**. While this curatorial process is intended to keep users engaged, it can also lead to **information manipulation**, as certain topics or viewpoints may be favoured over others.

11.3.2 Amplification of Misinformation

One of the most concerning aspects of algorithmic curation is the amplification of **misinformation**. Content that triggers strong emotional reactions, such as outrage or fear, tends to perform well in terms of engagement. Algorithms may, therefore, prioritise sensational or misleading content, leading to the rapid spread of **false information** and the distortion of public understanding. This phenomenon is particularly prevalent in times of crisis, such as during elections or public health emergencies.

11.3.3 The Role of Paid Content

Beyond organic content, algorithms also promote **paid advertisements** and sponsored posts, allowing individuals and organisations to pay for increased visibility. While this creates opportunities for businesses, it also opens the door for **manipulative actors** to push specific agendas or influence public opinion through targeted advertising. Political campaigns, for example, may use paid ads to manipulate voters by showing them carefully curated messages designed to exploit their biases or fears.

11.4 Manipulating Perception Through Visual and Emotional Cues

11.4.1 The Power of Visual Content

Images and videos have a profound impact on how we perceive reality. On social media, visual content often evokes stronger emotional responses than text, making it a powerful tool for influencing opinions. Manipulative actors can use **doctored images**, **deepfakes**, or **selective editing** to shape users' understanding of events, sometimes presenting fictionalised versions of reality as fact. As a result, users may form opinions based on misleading or false representations.

11.4.2 Emotional Manipulation and Clickbait

Social media platforms often capitalise on **emotional manipulation** to increase user engagement. **Clickbait** headlines and emotionally charged content are designed to provoke strong reactions, such as anger, sadness, or joy. These emotional triggers can distort users' perceptions, leading them to believe exaggerated claims or buy into narratives that are not entirely accurate. By consistently exposing users to emotionally charged content, social media platforms can subtly manipulate how they perceive issues, events, or people.

11.5 Social Validation and the Reinforcement of Norms

11.5.1 The Influence of Social Proof

Social proof is the psychological phenomenon where people assume the actions of others reflect the correct behaviour in a given situation. On social media, **likes**, **shares**, and **comments** serve as forms of social proof, influencing how users interpret content. Posts that receive high engagement are perceived as more credible or valuable, regardless of their accuracy. This leads to the amplification of certain ideas, further reinforcing users' beliefs.

11.5.2 Manipulating Trends and Norms

Through the use of social proof, social media platforms can shape **cultural norms** and dictate what is considered popular or acceptable. Trending topics, viral challenges, and influencer endorsements create a sense of what is "in," driving users to conform to these norms. Manipulative actors, including advertisers and political organisations, can exploit this to push products, ideas, or agendas that benefit them.

11.5.3 The Role of Influencers in Shaping Perception

Influencers wield significant power over public perception. Their large followings and perceived authenticity make them highly influential in shaping opinions, from product recommendations to political beliefs. Brands and organisations often leverage influencers to subtly manipulate public perception by associating their products or messages with trusted figures, creating the illusion of organic endorsement.

11.6 Information Overload: Diluting Critical Thinking

11.6.1 The Challenge of Information Overload

The sheer volume of information on social media can be overwhelming, leading to **information overload**. With constant updates, breaking news, and a stream of new posts, users are bombarded with content, making it difficult to discern fact from fiction. This overload can hinder critical thinking, as users may resort to **superficial engagement** with information, relying on quick impressions rather than deep analysis.

11.6.2 The Impact on Decision-Making

Information overload can have a profound effect on **decision-making**. Faced with too much information, users may experience **decision fatigue**, leading them to make snap judgments or rely on **heuristics** (mental shortcuts) when processing information. This makes them more susceptible to **cognitive biases** and manipulation, as they are less likely to critically evaluate the content they encounter.

11.7 The Role of Misinformation in Manipulating Public Perception

11.7.1 The Spread of Fake News

Fake news is one of the most pervasive forms of misinformation on social media. False or misleading stories are often spread to manipulate public perception, either for political gain or to sow discord. The **virality** of fake news is driven by algorithms that prioritise engaging content, leading to its rapid dissemination. In some cases, fake news is designed to look like legitimate journalism, making it difficult for users to distinguish between fact and fiction.

11.7.2 Manipulating Public Opinion

Misinformation campaigns are often orchestrated by **state actors**, **interest groups**, or **political organisations** to manipulate public opinion on key issues. These campaigns may involve the spread of false information, doctored media, or misleading statistics to create confusion or sway public sentiment. The ability to manipulate perception through misinformation is a powerful tool in shaping elections, public policy, and societal debates.

11.8 Conclusion: Navigating the Manipulation of Perception on Social Media

Social media platforms have a profound impact on how we perceive and understand the world around us. Through the use of algorithms, visual content, emotional manipulation, and social proof, these platforms can subtly shape our perceptions, reinforcing biases and limiting exposure to diverse viewpoints. Recognising the tools and tactics used to manipulate perception is critical to developing media literacy and becoming more discerning users of social media.

In the next chapter, **Chapter 12: Social Media and Manipulation in Advertising: Selling More Than Products**, we will explore how advertisers exploit social media platforms to influence consumer behaviour, using targeted ads, emotional manipulation, and social proof to sell more than just products.

Chapter 12: Social Media and Manipulation in Advertising: Selling More Than Products

12.1 Introduction: The Hidden Power of Social Media Advertising

Social media has transformed the advertising landscape, providing advertisers with unprecedented access to detailed user data, behavioural insights, and powerful targeting tools. While traditional advertising sought to sell products or services, social media advertising goes beyond this—it manipulates **perceptions**, **attitudes**, and **lifestyles**. In this chapter, we will explore how advertisers use targeted ads, emotional manipulation, and social proof to influence consumer behaviour, often selling more than just products. We will delve into the ethical implications of these techniques and their impact on individuals and society.

12.2 The Evolution of Advertising: From Billboards to Algorithms

12.2.1 Traditional Advertising vs. Social Media Advertising

Before the rise of social media, advertisers used traditional channels such as television, radio, and print to reach broad audiences. These methods were **generalised**, and while effective, they lacked the precision to target individual consumers based on their specific preferences and behaviours.

Social media has revolutionised advertising by introducing **algorithm-driven targeting** that can pinpoint users based on their age, location, interests, online behaviour, and more. This allows advertisers to craft highly personalised messages that are more likely to resonate with specific individuals, increasing the likelihood of successful persuasion.

12.2.2 The Role of Big Data in Advertising

Social media platforms gather vast amounts of data on users, tracking everything from the pages they visit to the ads they click on. This **big data** is invaluable to advertisers, who use it to create detailed profiles of users and predict their behaviour. By analysing this data, advertisers can tailor ads to specific individuals, exploiting their preferences, fears, and desires to maximise impact.

12.3 Targeted Ads: Precision Manipulation

12.3.1 How Targeted Ads Work

Targeted advertising uses algorithms to deliver ads to users who are most likely to engage with them. These algorithms consider factors such as past online behaviour, demographics, and interests to determine which ads to show. This level of precision allows advertisers to manipulate users by showing them ads that align with their personal preferences, making the ads seem relevant and tailored to their needs.

12.3.2 Exploiting Personal Data

The key to the effectiveness of targeted ads lies in the collection and analysis of personal data. Social media platforms use data such as browsing history, social media activity, and even location information to build detailed profiles of users. These profiles allow advertisers to craft **personalised messages** that appeal to specific emotions or desires, increasing the likelihood of a purchase or desired behaviour change.

12.3.3 The Ethical Dilemma of Personalised Ads

While targeted ads can enhance the user experience by making ads more relevant, they also raise ethical concerns. The use of personal data for advertising purposes blurs the line between **personal choice** and **manipulation**. Users may not realise how much of their data is being used to shape their experiences, leading to concerns about privacy, consent, and the manipulative nature of personalised advertising.

12.4 Emotional Manipulation in Advertising: Triggering Responses

12.4.1 The Role of Emotion in Advertising

Emotion is a powerful tool in advertising, and social media platforms have perfected the art of **emotional manipulation**. Advertisers use emotionally charged images, music, and messages to evoke feelings such as happiness, fear, or excitement. These emotions create a connection between the consumer and the product, making the consumer more likely to engage with the brand or make a purchase.

12.4.2 Fear and Scarcity Tactics

Advertisers often use **fear** and **scarcity** to manipulate consumers. Fear-based ads may highlight the potential dangers of not using a product (e.g., security software), while scarcity tactics create a sense of urgency by suggesting that a product is in limited supply or only available for a short time. These tactics play on consumers' emotions, driving them to act quickly and impulsively without fully considering their options.

12.4.3 Emotional Appeal in Cause Marketing

In recent years, advertisers have increasingly used **cause marketing**, where brands associate themselves with social or environmental causes. These campaigns appeal to users' emotions by aligning the brand with issues that resonate with their values. While cause marketing can be a force for good, it can also be manipulative, as some brands use these emotional appeals to distract from unethical practices or to create an illusion of social responsibility.

12.5 Social Proof: Influencing Through Others

12.5.1 What is Social Proof?

Social proof is the psychological phenomenon where people look to others to determine what is correct or desirable. On social media, **likes**, **shares**, **comments**, and **follower counts** serve as forms of social proof, influencing users' perceptions of products, brands, and even ideas. Advertisers leverage social proof to make their products or services seem more popular, credible, and desirable.

12.5.2 The Role of Influencers in Advertising

Influencers play a significant role in social proof. By endorsing products or services, influencers create the illusion of organic approval, making it seem as though they genuinely believe in what they are promoting. This form of advertising can be highly manipulative, as followers may not realise that influencers are being paid to promote certain products. Influencers often blur the line between personal recommendation and paid advertisement, making it difficult for users to discern when they are being marketed to.

12.5.3 Viral Campaigns and Manipulation of Trends

Advertisers also capitalise on **viral content** and **trending topics** to manipulate consumer behaviour. By creating campaigns that encourage users to participate, such as viral challenges or hashtag campaigns, advertisers tap into the power of social proof and FOMO (fear of missing out). These campaigns create a sense of **social obligation**, where users feel pressured to engage with the brand or product to fit in with their peers.

12.6 Manipulating Values and Lifestyles

12.6.1 Selling Aspirations

Social media advertising often sells more than just products—it sells **lifestyles** and **aspirations**. Advertisers craft messages that tap into consumers' desires for success, beauty, or happiness, suggesting that these ideals can be achieved through the purchase of specific products. By aligning products with aspirational goals, advertisers manipulate consumers into believing that their self-worth or happiness is tied to material goods.

12.6.2 The Rise of the "Curated Life"

Social media platforms have popularised the concept of the **curated life**, where users present idealised versions of themselves to their followers. Advertisers exploit this trend by promoting products that promise to enhance the curated lifestyle, from beauty products to luxury experiences. This manipulation reinforces the idea that one's value is determined by appearances and possessions, driving consumerism and increasing the pressure to conform to certain standards.

12.7 Ethical Considerations: Balancing Manipulation and Consumer Choice

12.7.1 The Thin Line Between Persuasion and Manipulation

While advertising has always been about persuasion, social media advertising crosses into the realm of **manipulation** when it exploits consumers' emotions, data, and social pressures to influence their behaviour. The distinction between persuasion and manipulation lies in the **intent** and **transparency** of the message. When advertisers intentionally obscure their motives or use deceptive tactics to influence consumers, they cross into unethical territory.

12.7.2 The Responsibility of Advertisers and Platforms

As social media continues to evolve, so too does the responsibility of advertisers and platforms. **Transparency**, **consent**, and **user protection** must be at the forefront of social media advertising practices. Platforms must ensure that users are aware of how their data is being used and that ads are clearly labelled. At the same time, advertisers must strike a balance between creativity and ethical responsibility, avoiding manipulative tactics that exploit vulnerable users.

12.8 Conclusion: The Hidden Impact of Social Media Advertising

Social media advertising is a powerful tool that goes beyond selling products—it manipulates consumer behaviour, emotions, and perceptions. Through targeted ads, emotional manipulation, and social proof, advertisers can subtly influence users' decisions, often without their full awareness. As consumers, it is important to recognise these tactics and develop **media literacy** to navigate the complexities of modern advertising.

In the next chapter, **Chapter 13: The Role of Regulation in Social Media Manipulation: Protecting Users or Stifling Innovation?**, we will explore the regulatory landscape surrounding social media and advertising, examining whether current regulations are sufficient to protect users from manipulation or if they hinder innovation in the digital economy.

Chapter 13: The Role of Regulation in Social Media Manipulation: Protecting Users or Stifling Innovation?

13.1 Introduction: The Need for Regulation in Social Media

As social media continues to evolve, so too do concerns over the **manipulative practices** employed by platforms and advertisers. The proliferation of **targeted ads**, **emotional manipulation**, and the use of **personal data** has led to widespread calls for **regulation** to protect users from undue influence and exploitation. However, critics argue that excessive regulation could stifle innovation, limit freedom of expression, and hinder the growth of the digital economy. In this chapter, we will explore the regulatory landscape surrounding social media and advertising, examining the delicate balance between protecting users and fostering innovation.

13.2 The Current Regulatory Framework

13.2.1 Existing Laws and Regulations

Across the world, different jurisdictions have established regulations aimed at protecting users from manipulation and ensuring transparency in advertising. In the **UK**, regulations are overseen by bodies such as the **Information Commissioner's**

Office (ICO) and the **Advertising Standards Authority (ASA)**. The **General Data Protection Regulation (GDPR)**, which applies across the European Union, sets strict rules on the collection, use, and protection of personal data, impacting how social media platforms handle user information.

In the United States, regulations like the **Federal Trade Commission (FTC) Act** oversee advertising practices, while specific states like **California** have implemented comprehensive privacy laws, such as the **California Consumer Privacy Act (CCPA)**.

13.2.2 Key Regulatory Principles

The key principles that guide current regulations are:

- **Transparency**: Ensuring users are aware of how their data is being collected and used.

- **Consent**: Users must give explicit permission for their data to be utilised for advertising purposes.

- **Accountability**: Platforms and advertisers are responsible for ensuring their practices comply with regulations and that users are protected from manipulation.

- **Data Protection**: Safeguarding personal data to prevent misuse or exploitation.

13.3 The Role of Regulators: Protecting Users from Manipulation

13.3.1 Addressing Privacy Concerns

One of the primary concerns that regulators focus on is **data privacy**. With social media platforms collecting vast amounts of personal data, there are growing fears about how this information is being used to manipulate user behaviour. Regulators seek to ensure that users have control over their data and that platforms are transparent about how this data is used in advertising and content delivery.

Regulations like GDPR place strict limits on what companies can do with user data, requiring **clear consent** and giving users the right to request the deletion of their data. These rules are designed to protect individuals from being unknowingly manipulated through their personal information.

13.3.2 Combatting Deceptive Advertising Practices

Regulators also focus on preventing **deceptive advertising** practices. This includes ensuring that ads are clearly identifiable as paid content, that influencer endorsements are disclosed, and that users are not misled by **dark patterns** or other manipulative design features. In the UK, the **ASA's guidelines** require advertisers to make clear distinctions between organic and sponsored content to avoid misleading consumers.

13.3.3 Tackling Fake News and Misinformation

The rise of **fake news** and **misinformation** on social media platforms has prompted regulators to take action. These false or misleading stories, often spread for financial gain or political manipulation, pose a significant threat to public discourse. Regulators are increasingly working to hold platforms accountable for the spread of misinformation, requiring them to implement fact-checking processes and remove harmful content.

13.4 Innovation and the Free Market: The Risks of Over-Regulation

13.4.1 Stifling Innovation

While regulation is necessary to protect users, critics argue that excessive regulation can **stifle innovation**. Social media platforms and advertisers rely on **data-driven innovation** to improve user experiences, create personalised content, and develop new business models. By imposing strict rules on data usage and advertising, governments risk **limiting the potential** of these platforms to evolve and improve.

For example, regulations that restrict **targeted advertising** could reduce the effectiveness of ads, leading to reduced revenue for platforms. This, in turn, could affect the ability of companies to offer free services or invest in new technologies like artificial intelligence (AI) and machine learning (ML).

13.4.2 The Impact on Small Businesses and Startups

Another concern is that regulatory compliance can be **costly**, especially for small businesses and startups. Major platforms like Facebook and Google may have the resources to comply with complex data protection laws, but smaller companies may struggle. This could lead to a **consolidation of power** among larger platforms, as smaller competitors find it difficult to navigate the regulatory environment.

Moreover, startups often rely on **personalised advertising** to reach their target audiences effectively. If these avenues are restricted, it could limit their ability to grow and compete in the market, reducing innovation in the digital economy.

13.5 Striking a Balance: Ethical Innovation

13.5.1 Responsible Innovation

While regulation is necessary to prevent exploitation, it is possible to **innovate responsibly** without stifling creativity. Platforms can implement **ethical practices** that prioritise user well-being and transparency while still allowing for data-driven innovation. For instance, they could provide clearer opt-in options for personalised ads, allow users greater control over their data, and design interfaces that are free from dark patterns.

By adopting **user-centric** approaches, platforms can continue to evolve while respecting users' rights and privacy.

13.5.2 Self-Regulation and Industry Standards

In addition to government regulation, there is growing interest in **self-regulation** within the industry. Social media platforms and advertising companies can take proactive steps to establish **ethical standards** and **best practices** that promote transparency and protect users from manipulation. By creating **voluntary codes of conduct**, platforms can demonstrate their commitment to responsible behaviour without waiting for government intervention.

Examples of self-regulation include **transparency reports** that detail how user data is handled and what steps are taken to combat misinformation. Industry associations can also establish **certification schemes** for ethical advertising, ensuring that businesses that meet high standards are recognised and trusted by users.

13.6 International Cooperation: The Challenge of Global Regulation

Social media is a global phenomenon, but **regulatory frameworks** vary by region. This presents a significant challenge when it comes to addressing social media manipulation. While countries like the UK and EU have strict regulations, others have more relaxed approaches, creating a patchwork of rules that platforms must navigate.

13.6.1 Harmonising Global Standards

There is growing recognition of the need for **international cooperation** to create consistent regulations that apply across borders. Organisations like the **United Nations** and the **World Economic Forum** have called for **global standards** that protect users from exploitation while supporting innovation. Harmonising regulations could help ensure that all users, regardless of location, are afforded the same protections.

13.6.2 The Role of Platforms in Global Compliance

Social media platforms must navigate this complex regulatory environment, balancing local laws with their global reach. Companies like Facebook, Twitter, and TikTok are increasingly adopting **global policies** to streamline compliance and ensure they meet the highest standards in all markets. However, this can lead to tension when platforms must adhere to **local laws** that may conflict with their global approach, such as censorship laws in certain countries.

13.7 Conclusion: Balancing Protection and Innovation

The regulation of social media manipulation is a **delicate balancing act**. On one hand, there is a clear need to protect users from exploitation, ensure transparency, and safeguard personal data. On the other hand, over-regulation risks stifling innovation, limiting the potential of platforms to evolve and create new opportunities.

The future of social media regulation will depend on the ability of governments, platforms, and industry stakeholders to collaborate in creating **flexible, adaptive** frameworks that protect users without hindering progress. Ultimately, the goal should be to foster a **digital economy** that is both **innovative** and **ethical**, ensuring that the power of social media is harnessed for the benefit of all.

In the next chapter, **Chapter 14: The Future of Social Media: Ethical Manipulation and User Empowerment**, we will explore how the future of social media could evolve to incorporate ethical design principles and empower users to take control of their digital experiences, ensuring a healthier balance between engagement and manipulation.

Chapter 14: The Future of Social Media: Ethical Manipulation and User Empowerment

14.1 Introduction: The Path Forward

As the role of social media continues to expand in everyday life, there is growing recognition of the need for **ethical approaches** to user engagement and manipulation. In recent years, public awareness of the negative effects of manipulative design practices has increased, sparking debates about how platforms can evolve in a way that **prioritises user well-being**. In this chapter, we will explore how the future of social media could incorporate **ethical design principles**, create a more **transparent user experience**, and **empower individuals** to take control of their interactions in the digital space.

14.2 Ethical Manipulation: Redefining Engagement

14.2.1 From Exploitation to Ethical Influence

The concept of **manipulation** doesn't inherently carry a negative connotation—when done ethically, it can guide users toward positive behaviours, such as adopting healthier habits or engaging in **constructive discussions**. Platforms can move away from exploiting user behaviour for profit and instead focus on **nudging** users toward actions that are **beneficial to them** and society.

For example, rather than using algorithms solely to keep users on the platform, social media could implement features that encourage **mindful usage**, such as **break reminders** and **time management tools**. Ethical manipulation would involve steering users away from harmful content or addictive behaviours, while still keeping them engaged.

14.2.2 Human-Centric Design: Prioritising User Well-being

A shift towards **human-centric design** would involve redesigning social media platforms to prioritise **user well-being** over time spent on the platform. This could involve giving users more **control over algorithms**, allowing them to tailor their feed to show content that aligns with their personal values and goals. Ethical manipulation would also involve **limiting the spread of harmful content**, focusing on creating **positive engagement loops**.

By incorporating **well-being metrics** into platform design, social media companies can track and improve how their platforms affect mental and emotional health, ensuring that users engage in more **balanced and fulfilling** interactions.

14.3 User Empowerment: Giving Control Back to the Users

14.3.1 Transparency and Choice: Allowing Users to Shape Their Experience

A crucial component of ethical social media will be **transparency**—users need to know exactly how algorithms work, what data is being collected, and how their behaviour is being shaped by the platform. Providing users with the **choice** to customise their social media experience can reduce the negative effects of manipulation and increase satisfaction.

14.3.2 Tools for Self-Regulation: Empowering Users to Manage Their Usage

One way to give control back to users is through the creation of tools that allow for **self-regulation**. These could include:

- **Customisable algorithms**: Users could adjust how content is prioritised in their feeds, choosing to see more posts from friends or educational content, for example.

- **Time management features**: Providing in-app analytics to show users how they spend their time on the platform, encouraging healthy habits by limiting time spent in unproductive loops.

- **Notification control**: Giving users the ability to better manage notifications, so they aren't constantly prompted to return to the app but only when content is important or personally relevant.

14.4 Designing for Empowerment: Case Studies and Emerging Trends

14.4.1 Ethical Platform Initiatives

Several social media platforms have already begun experimenting with features that promote **ethical engagement**. For instance, some platforms now offer **well-being checks** that prompt users to take breaks or provide resources for mental health when certain behaviours are detected.

Platforms like **YouTube** have added features to reduce manipulation, such as turning off **autoplay** by default for users who don't opt in. Similarly, **Instagram** has tested features to remove public like counts, reducing the focus on popularity and fostering a healthier environment for self-expression.

14.4.2 Emerging Technologies for User Empowerment

Blockchain technology and **decentralised social media** are gaining traction as tools for empowering users. Blockchain-based platforms allow users to retain

control over their data, ensuring that their information is not being harvested without consent. These platforms offer **transparency** and **ownership**, which could lead to a fundamental shift in how users interact with social media.

Additionally, advancements in **artificial intelligence (AI)** could allow platforms to create more sophisticated tools for user empowerment. For example, **AI-driven personalisation** could give users more control over what content they see without exposing them to unwanted manipulation or advertising. This would enable a future where users can **actively shape** their own digital landscapes.

14.5 Ethical Manipulation in Advertising: A New Era of Consumer Trust

14.5.1 Ethical Advertising Practices

As the public becomes more aware of manipulation techniques, advertisers will need to adopt **ethical marketing practices** to build consumer trust. This could involve **clear disclosures** of sponsored content, removing deceptive techniques, and ensuring that ads are relevant and non-invasive.

14.5.2 Empowering Users Through Ethical Ad Controls

Future social media platforms could offer users the ability to **opt-in** to certain types of advertising, creating a more transparent relationship between consumers and brands. By giving users more control over the ads they see, platforms can foster an environment where **trust** and **engagement** are prioritised over manipulation and profit maximisation.

14.6 The Role of Policy Makers: Supporting Ethical Innovation

Governments and regulatory bodies will need to support these innovations by creating frameworks that **encourage ethical practices** without stifling creativity or growth. Policymakers should focus on:

- **Encouraging transparency** from platforms on how their algorithms work and what data is collected.

- **Promoting user education** on how to engage critically with social media.

- Supporting research and innovation in ethical technology, providing incentives for platforms that adopt **pro-social behaviours** in their design.

14.7 Conclusion: A Vision for the Future

The future of social media holds tremendous potential for positive change, but it will require a commitment to **ethical manipulation** and **user empowerment**. By integrating **human-centric design**, **transparent practices**, and **user-controlled experiences**, social media platforms can transform into spaces that promote **well-being** while still fostering **engagement**.

Empowering users with the tools to shape their digital experiences, while holding platforms accountable for their practices, will lead to a healthier balance between **innovation** and **ethics** in the evolving social media landscape. The question is no longer whether social media will shape our world, but how it will do so in a way that benefits both individuals and society as a whole.

Chapter 14: Strategies for Users to Recognize and Resist Manipulation

14.1 Identifying Manipulative Tactics on Social Media

Social media platforms employ various manipulative tactics that can easily go unnoticed. Recognising these tactics is the first step towards resisting manipulation.

- **Fear of Missing Out (FOMO)**: Platforms often leverage FOMO by creating a sense of urgency. This can manifest through limited-time offers, countdown timers, and notifications about trending content. Users may feel compelled to engage quickly, often making impulsive decisions. For example, social media advertisements may highlight "only 5 items left!" to push users to act without fully considering their choices.

- **Confirmation Bias**: Algorithms are designed to show users content that aligns with their beliefs, which can lead to a narrow view of the world. For example, if a user frequently engages with political content that reinforces their views, the platform will likely continue to show similar content. This creates echo chambers, making it essential for users to intentionally seek out diverse opinions and sources to gain a balanced perspective.

- **Emotional Appeals**: Many posts and advertisements use emotionally charged language or imagery to provoke strong reactions, whether anger, joy, or sadness. This emotional manipulation can lead users to share content without critical analysis. Users should be aware of their emotional responses when engaging with content and take a step back to evaluate the underlying message.

- **Social Proof**: Platforms often showcase popular content based on likes, shares, and comments, suggesting that widely endorsed posts are more credible. This can manipulate users into accepting the majority viewpoint without question. It's crucial for users to question why something is popular and whether it aligns with their values and beliefs.

Developing critical thinking and media literacy is essential for navigating the digital world effectively.

- **Evaluating Sources**: Users should learn to assess the credibility of sources by checking the author's credentials, looking for citations, and verifying claims through multiple sources. Tools such as fact-checking websites (e.g., Snopes, FactCheck.org) can assist in this process. Additionally, recognising the difference between news articles, opinion pieces, and sponsored content can help users make informed choices.

- **Understanding Bias**: Users should be aware of potential biases in the information presented, whether through the lens of the platform or the content creator. Being able to identify whether a source has a specific agenda or bias will help users to discern the reliability of the information they encounter. It's essential to cultivate a habit of questioning the motives behind the information being shared.

- **Reflective Consumption**: Encourage users to pause and reflect before sharing content, considering its accuracy and the motivations behind its creation. Asking questions such as, "What is the source of this information?" or "What impact does sharing this have?" can help cultivate a more thoughtful approach to social media interactions.

14.3 Understanding the Impact of Algorithms on Your Content

Users should understand how algorithms shape their experiences on social media.

- **Algorithmic Filters**: Discuss how algorithms prioritise content based on user engagement and past behaviour. For example, if a user interacts predominantly with posts about fitness, their feed may become saturated with similar content, limiting exposure to other topics. Understanding this can help users recognise the limitations of their feeds and the need for deliberate diversification.

- **Adjusting Settings**: Provide guidance on how users can adjust their settings to diversify their feed, such as following a wider range of accounts, adjusting their preferences, or turning off engagement tracking. Many platforms allow users to modify what content they see by unfollowing accounts that do not provide value or turning on features that highlight diverse content.

- **Transparency Initiatives**: Highlight platforms' efforts (or lack thereof) in promoting transparency about how algorithms operate and the data they use. Discuss any recent moves by social media companies to provide users with insights into how their content is curated. This awareness can empower users to take control of their online experiences.

14.4 How to Take Control of Your Social Media Usage

Empower users with strategies to manage their social media usage intentionally.

- **Setting Time Limits**: Encourage users to set boundaries on their social media time to prevent addictive behaviours and promote healthier habits. Using built-in features on smartphones and apps that track and limit usage can be an effective way to ensure users do not exceed their desired limits. It's important to set specific time frames for social media engagement, allowing for more focused and intentional use.

- **Mindful Engagement**: Advise users to engage with content purposefully, focusing on quality over quantity in their interactions. Encourage practices such as reflecting on why they are sharing a post or taking a moment to think about its relevance to their lives and values. Mindfulness can help users to engage in a more meaningful way, ultimately enhancing their social media experience.

- **Utilising Tools and Features**: Provide information on tools that help users monitor their usage patterns and identify harmful behaviours, such as screen time trackers. Many platforms now offer insights into user activity, allowing individuals to understand their habits better. Encourage users to regularly review these insights and adjust their usage based on their findings.

Chapter 15: Conclusion: The Future of Social Media and Manipulation

15.1 The Evolution of Social Media Manipulation Tactics

Reflecting on the chapters covered, this section summarises the evolution of manipulation tactics used by social media platforms.

- **Historical Context**: Briefly discuss how manipulation tactics have evolved alongside technological advancements, from simple advertisements to sophisticated algorithms and emotional manipulation. For example, the introduction of targeted advertising based on user data has dramatically changed how brands connect with consumers, moving from broad messaging to highly personalised campaigns.

- **Adapting to Change**: Emphasise the importance of staying informed about emerging manipulation techniques as technology continues to evolve. This includes being aware of trends such as deepfakes, AI-generated content, and new social media platforms that may utilise different manipulation strategies.

15.2 Potential Solutions: Regulatory and Ethical Considerations

This section examines the regulatory landscape and ethical considerations that can mitigate manipulation.

- **The Role of Governments**: Discuss how regulatory bodies can implement measures to protect users, such as enforcing transparency requirements for algorithms and data usage. Highlight recent legislative efforts, such as the European Union's General Data Protection Regulation (GDPR), which aims to protect user data and privacy rights.

- **Ethical Design Practices**: Highlight the need for social media companies to adopt ethical design practices, prioritising user well-being over profit. This can include designing interfaces that do not exploit vulnerabilities and instead encourage healthy engagement with content.

- **Public Awareness Campaigns**: Advocate for campaigns that promote awareness of manipulative tactics, equipping users with the knowledge to recognise and resist them. These campaigns could be spearheaded by educational institutions, non-profits, and government agencies, fostering a culture of digital literacy and critical engagement.

15.3 Balancing Innovation and Manipulation: What's Next for Social Media

Consider the balance between innovation in social media and the potential for manipulation.

- **The Innovation-Integrity Balance**: Discuss the importance of finding a balance between innovative engagement techniques and ethical user treatment. Companies must consider the long-term consequences of their design choices and the potential for exploitation.

- **Future Trends**: Speculate on future trends in social media, such as increased personalisation, emerging platforms, and the potential impact of artificial intelligence. Discuss how these trends could either enhance user experiences or exacerbate manipulative practices, depending on how they are implemented.

15.4 Empowering Users in the Age of Digital Manipulation

Conclude with a call to action for user empowerment in navigating social media manipulation.

- **Encouraging Agency**: Encourage users to take an active role in their social media experiences, from critically assessing content to engaging in dialogue about ethical practices. This can involve participating in discussions about algorithm transparency and advocating for changes that promote user agency.

- **Community Building**: Advocate for the importance of building communities that support informed engagement, fostering environments where critical discussions about manipulation can take place. This includes encouraging users to share their experiences and strategies for resisting manipulation.

- **Ongoing Education**: Emphasise the need for continual learning about digital literacy, urging users to stay informed about changes in social media landscapes and manipulation tactics. Educational resources, workshops, and online courses can equip users with the necessary skills to navigate the digital world more effectively.

www.ingramcontent.com/pod-product-compliance
Lightning Source LLC
LaVergne TN
LVHW062035060326
832903LV00062B/1688